HOPE: THE HEART'S GREAT QUEST

HOPE:
The Heart's Great Quest

DAVID AIKMAN

Servant Publications
Ann Arbor, Michigan

Vine Books is an imprint of Servant Publications especially designed to serve evangelical Christians.

All Scripture quotations, unless indicated, are taken from the *Holy Bible, New International Version*. © 1973, 1978, 1984 by International Bible Society. Used by permission of Zondervan Publishing House. All rights reserved.

Published by Servant Publications
P.O. Box 8617
Ann Arbor, Michigan 48107

Cover design by Multnomah Graphics, Portland, Oregon

95 96 97 98 99 10 9 8 7 6 5 4 3 2 1

Printed in the United States of America
ISBN 0-89283-793-4

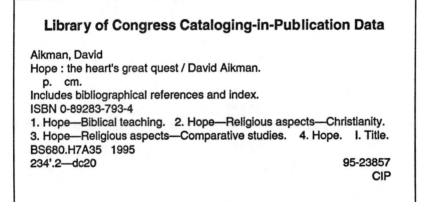

Library of Congress Cataloging-in-Publication Data

Aikman, David
Hope : the heart's great quest / David Aikman.
   p.   cm.
Includes bibliographical references and index.
ISBN 0-89283-793-4
1. Hope—Biblical teaching.   2. Hope—Religious aspects—Christianity.
3. Hope—Religious aspects—Comparative studies.   4. Hope.   I. Title.
BS680.H7A35   1995
234'.2—dc20   95-23857
                                                                   CIP

Contents

ONE

Hope Is Everywhere

It was January 17, 1991, the very first day of Operation Desert Storm. After months of careful buildup, U.S. and allied forces operating out of Saudi Arabia had started a full-scale air assault upon Iraqi military positions in Kuwait and Iraq itself. Among the most hazardous of the air strikes: low-level attacks on highly defended Iraqi airfields by British Tornado fighter-bombers.

The Tornado was designed to operate best at night in this attack mode, but for a variety of reasons the flight of three aircraft, each with its two-man crew, was hurtling across the desert floor of Iraq in broad daylight. For Flight Lieutenant John Peters, the pilot of one of the Tornadoes, and his navigator, Flight Lieutenant John Nichol, it was their first taste ever of real wartime combat.

It was also their last. As they pulled up from their attacking altitude of barely fifty feet, flying at nearly 600 miles per hour, an Iraqi SAM missile plowed into their engine tailpipe, exploding with a force that caused the entire aircraft to shudder and forced the two men to eject into the heart of enemy territory.

Their parachutes let them land gently enough to avoid injury, and for a few moments the two of them burst into laughter, relieved to be miraculously alive, and struck by the absurdity and vulnerability of their position. But then an Iraqi patrol spotted them and began moving rapidly across the sand toward their position. Bursts of automatic fire buzzed through the air above them and tore into the ground nearby. Frantically, they clawed down into the sand to get out of the line of fire—anything to avoid the terrible impact of those bullets. For a few brief moments, fearing the agony of possible torture by their Iraqi captors, they contemplated mutual suicide.

"I looked at John [Peters]," John Nichol recounts in their best-selling story of the incident, titled *Tornado Down*.

"Now when it came right down to it, I didn't much fancy killing him, in any case. It seemed absurd; we had known each other for a long time. I was much less than sure I could do it. There was another option, though.

"'Look,' I said. 'They are going to come and get us anyway. Shall we go out with a bang?' I was suggesting that we start shooting back at them, make a fight of it at least. It looked like they were going to kill us anyway.

"Dazedly, he looked at the gun I was aiming at the skirmish line. 'No, there's always hope,' he said, with a warmth in his voice I was surprised to hear. I looked over to him, and he smiled, wryly. All of a sudden, I knew he was right."[1]

He *was* right. The two men survived the fusillade of shooting without being hit, surrendered to the Iraqi soldiers, and were held for the remaining few weeks of the war as P.O.W.s. They were beaten up, threatened with death, nearly killed by other allied bombing raids. Yet they survived, were released, and recovered from their ordeal.

Hope. Always hope.

WHILE THERE'S LIFE, THERE'S HOPE

You can hardly get through a single day without hearing or reading the word *hope*—or saying it yourself. "I hope it doesn't rain," we remark, looking out of the car window dismally as dark clouds loom over the nice meadow we've selected for our picnic.

"I hope the check arrives tomorrow," the young entrepreneur mutters as he thinks of money long owed that has now become vital to keep his family afloat for another week.

"I hope you have a really great time," says the mother to her college-bound son, suppressing her own anxieties over the young man's first real flight from the family nest as much as assuaging his trepidation.

More menacingly, the boss pokes his head in the door and crisply declares to the employee: "I hope you get that project done by the deadline."

The word *hope* fills our newspapers, our politicians' speeches, and every expressed yearning of our life. "At Inauguration, Mayor Pledges Era of Hope," intones a *New York Times* headline as newly elected Rudolph Giuliani takes the oath of office on a brisk January morning in New York City.

"All We Can Do Is Pray and Hope," says the boldface from the *Atlanta Constitution,* citing Mayor Pat Gibbs of Davenport, Iowa, as the Midwest floodwaters infiltrate his town's defenses.

"Our Commitment Is Haiti's Best Hope," declares *The Washington Post,* quoting a Florida senator. Or, "Hope Stings Eternal," mocks the same paper in its Style section on a different day, wryly telling the story of an unorthodox self-help group of multiple sclerosis sufferers that specializes in therapy using bee sting venom.

E*ither we have hope within us or we don't; it is a dimension of the soul and it's not essentially dependent on some particular observation of the world or estimate of the situation.*

Our dictionaries and thesauruses are no less well stocked with examples of the word *hope.* The overwhelming majority are encouraging and edifying, aphorisms from some of the greatest names in Western culture and history, folk sayings offering a remedy for fear, grief, or despair culled from myriad languages and cultures.

"While there's life, there's hope" is perhaps the best-known and best-loved saying on hope in the English language. It reflects the deepest instinct of all human beings, regardless of nation or culture—the desire to survive. It has become an English proverb, but it was originally borrowed from Cicero, who may himself have taken it from the Latin playwright Terence (190-159 B.C.). Cicero reported that it was commonly said to sick people in his day, more than two millennia ago.

"Hope does not disappoint us," says the Bible (Romans 5:5), which is the Christian version of another phrase from literature that has entered everyday English speech: "Hope springs eternal." The quotation, appropriately enough, comes from Alexander Pope's *An Essay on Man.*

Quotations rich in the word *hope* fill our history books, especially in America, which foreign observers have always seen as a nation uniquely characterized by a sense of unquenchable hope. America's most beloved president, Abraham Lincoln, at a time of deep national crisis during the

Civil War, referred to America in his second annual message to Congress in stirring terms that have become etched in the national memory. Of the ultimate stakes involved in the battle for the soul of the U.S. in the Civil War, Lincoln said quite simply: "We shall nobly save or meanly lose the last, best hope of earth."

HAVEL'S VIEW OF HOPE

This intuitive sense of hope is one of the great sources of true courage available to men and women in the political arena. No modern statesman has grasped it more illuminatingly than Vaclav Havel, the brilliant and deeply humane president of the Czech Republic. For years an opposition writer and teacher whose championship of truth and human rights landed him in jail several times (a total of nearly five years), Havel has always understood something profound about the nature of political power: to be willing to embrace change, voters or even disenfranchised citizens must be persuaded that the change will bring something they can truly put their hope in.

Havel's political philosophy, during the years of Communist control, was almost anarchic in its refusal to accept conventional constraints, at least in the view of many of his friends. The only essential thing an individual could do to oppose totalitarianism, he insisted, was not to subscribe either publicly or privately to the lies or corruption essential to keep the system in power.

Havel, like many other Czechs, and like countless dissidents in many Communist countries, paid the price for such integrity: He experienced harassment, professional discrimination, public vilification, and imprisonment. To a person of limited vision, the gestures were pointless and doomed to accomplish nothing. He was indeed considered quixotic.

Yet Havel was no dreamer with his head in the clouds. By understanding that truth was freedom's secret weapon, and by refusing to be co-opted by "reasonable" compromises offered by the regime ("Just keep your critical words to a small group of friends, and you can travel abroad as much as you like"), Havel laid bare the deep vulnerability of authorities who didn't know how to cope with dissenters unafraid of the consequences of their protest. In the process, he helped bring down the Communist government that tried to suppress his dissent.

Havel's secret? A political behavior to which he devotes an entire chapter in his book *Disturbing the Peace* (New York: Vintage Books, 1990). He calls it "The Politics of Hope." In the excerpt below, Havel answers a question by the book's interviewer, Karel Hvizdala, on whether he sees any "grain of hope" in a world that still appears greatly at risk from Communist subversion, unchecked war, and the brutalization of life in the twentieth century. Havel's interesting reply:

> I should probably say first that the kind of hope I often think about (especially in situations that are particularly hopeless, such as prison), I understand above all as a state of mind, not a state of the world. Either we have hope within us or we don't; it is a dimension of the soul and it's not essentially dependent on some particular observation of the world or estimate of the situation. Hope is not prognostication. It is an orientation of the spirit, an orientation of the heart; it transcends the world that is immediately experienced, and is anchored somewhere beyond its horizons. I don't think you can explain it as a mere derivative of something here, or some movement, or of some favorable signs in the world. I feel that its deepest roots are in the transcendental, just as the roots of human responsibility are....[2]

Havel acknowledges almost wistfully that he himself lacks formal religious beliefs. Yet his understanding of the transcendental—something that has a spiritual dimension not measurable in normal materialistic terms—is in a way profoundly religious. For Havel, hope is a universal quality, at least potentially, of the human spirit as a whole. He continues:

> Hope, in this deep and powerful sense, is not the same as joy that things are going well, or willingness to invest in enterprises that are obviously headed for early success, but, rather, an ability to work for something because it is good, not just because it stands a chance to succeed. The more unpropitious the situation in which we demonstrate hope, the deeper that hope is. Hope is definitely not the same thing as optimism. It is not the conviction that something will turn out well, but the certainty that something makes sense, regardless of how it turns out.[3]

For Havel this understanding of hope was a beacon of sanity in a society made dark by mendacity, corruption, hypocrisy, and public folly under Communist Party rule. Hope inspired Havel to live a life of integrity in a society that seemed determined not to honor it.

HOPE AND HEALING

Even more fundamentally, hope has literally breathed health into sick people, life into the dying, and sanity into the mentally ill. In a virtual explosion of studies from the 1960s onward, medical research has demonstrated over and over an insight that poets, artists, and acute observers of human nature of all kinds have intuitively understood for centuries. This is that, just as deep disappointments can shock people into actual sickness, so exciting good news can sometimes bring rapid recovery from certain kinds of illness. "Hope deferred makes the heart sick," says King Solomon (Prv 13:12). Conversely, he reminds us two chapters later, "Good news gives health to the bones" (Prv 15:30).

While much of this might seem so self-evident as not to require comment, for a long time scientists and physicians resisted efforts to demonstrate the phenomenon scientifically. Perhaps they worried that the "scientific" side of medicine, with its reliance on measurability, predictability, and repeatability, might be compromised by delving into

H*ope has literally breathed health into sick people, life into the dying and sanity into the mentally ill.*

such subjective areas of research as human feelings. Yet, as Martin Seligman points out in *Learned Optimism: How to Change Your Mind and Your Life,* "In the last five years, laboratories around the world have produced a steady flow of scientific evidence that psychological traits, particularly optimism, can produce good health."[4]

From the late 1960s onwards, the number of studies demonstrating the connection between positive emotional states and a healthy physiology has grown steadily, with the investigations spread equally among the purely physical aspects of health and the largely mental. At the Virginia Commonwealth University in Richmond, Timothy R. Elliott, a counseling psychologist, studied patients who had suffered nearly identical injuries to the spinal cord in the prime of their lives.

Elliott found that the hopeful patients were less likely to be depressed, were able to move around better, and even had more fulfilling sex lives than those who couldn't find any new purpose for their lives. Elliott has said that many of the patients who belonged in the hopeful category had interpreted their injury as having a purpose in their lives that gave them a whole new challenge.[5]

Another researcher, M.F. Scheier, discovered that middle-aged men recovering from heart bypass surgery had a faster rate of physical healing during hospitalization, a quicker hospital discharge rate, and a tendency to return to normal activities after surgery sooner, if their disposition was optimistic.[6] In a separate finding, cardiologists Meyer Friedman and Diane Ulmer demonstrated how anger-prone, Type A heart attack survivors in the San Francisco area experienced half as many repeat heart attacks as a control group when they were counseled to relax, laugh at themselves, admit mistakes, and renew their religious faith.[7]

HOPE THROUGH LOVING CARE

And what of those for whom not even the very best medicine can offer the postponement of death? Even as medicine has shown the beneficial effects of hope upon the sick who may be capable of recovery, one individual has demonstrated the power of hope to transform the lives of those who are unquestionably dying.

Probably no person in our century has given that sense of hope to more people than Mother Teresa of Calcutta, a saintly Albanian nun who, with her Missionaries of Charity, has dedicated her life to ministering to the dying and the outcast on the streets of Calcutta. At the National Prayer Breakfast in Washington, D.C., in February 1994, in the presence of President Bill Clinton, Vice President Al Gore, and thousands of government officials, foreign diplomats, and other dignitaries, Mother Teresa described the smiles that would come over the faces of those she had picked up from the streets just moments before they died.

"She gave me much more," she said of one woman who was close to death when the sisters found her on the streets of Calcutta, "and she died with a smile on her face." What Mother Teresa did not say, but that was obvious, was that she and her sisters had brought the reality of Christ's love to her "incurable" patients so powerfully that the imminent sense of heaven became inescapable to them. And it was the anticipation of heaven—the hope—that brought them such joy at the very end of their lives.

If hope promotes healing for those within physiological reach of healing and joy for those beyond it, hope's antithesis, despair, or simply pessimism, seems to attract illness as bad news attracts gossips. Christopher Peterson, Ph.D., a psychologist at the University of Michigan, administered a test on a scale of optimism/pessimism devised by another psychologist, Martin Seligman, to 172 male and female students during the 1980s.

Tracking their health records over many years, Peterson found that those in the pessimistic segment of the scale had twice as many colds, sore throats, and flu outbreaks as the optimists and made twice as many visits to the doctor. Seligman himself supervised experiments that also demonstrated that pessimistic people were far more likely to become depressed than others.[8]

WHEN HOPE IS LOST

The sudden withdrawal of hope among people with serious illnesses, in fact, can lead to a rapid deterioration in their conditions and to death itself. In a frequently cited case from the 1950s, the psychologist Bruno Klopfer described how a certain Mr. Wright, a patient with an untreatable cancer that had spread throughout his body, had responded with astonishing speed to a new and experimental drug called Krebiozen. Mr. Wright had implored the doctors to administer the drug even though it was thought to be effective, if at all, only with less seriously ill patients. The doctors had consented reluctantly.

Mr. Wright continued to be well until press reports came out two months later questioning the effectiveness of Krebiozen. He then deteriorated rapidly to his original condition. At this point, Klopfer decided on a gentle subterfuge that he suspected might help the patient. He assured Mr. Wright that Krebiozen worked but that the original drug shipments had been spoiled through improper storage. He then had the patient injected with water that he described as part of a "new shipment" of Krebiozen. Once again, Mr. Wright got better, this time more rapidly than after the original, real Krebiozen.

But medical truth yet again intervened. It was impossible to insulate Mr. Wright from news stories two months later not simply questioning Krebiozen but declaring it to be medically worthless in the treatment of cancer. Unfortunately, within a few days of this bad news, Mr. Wright was readmitted to the hospital in serious physical condition. Klopfer wrote: "His faith was now gone, his last hope vanished, and he succumbed in less than two days."[9]

Aside from the questionable wisdom—not to mention the debatable ethics—of deliberately misleading a patient about a drug when the patient was fully capable of reading newspaper reports about it himself, the Wright-Krebiozen incident shows in an extreme way just how hope alone can keep a person physically alive.

If hope is such a concrete element in human consciousness, can it be measured in a scientific sense?

THE HOPE SCALE

One researcher who has concluded that it can be is Dr. Charles Snyder of the University of Kansas. During a sabbatical from his regular faculty job at the university, Snyder found himself reading deeply in the literature of survivors of deep adversity, including former prison camp inmates, the bereaved, or those with suddenly acquired physical handicaps.

Two characteristics were evident in these people, Snyder discovered: an intense desire to accomplish a certain goal, and the belief that the means could somehow be found to do so. Snyder came to describe this "cognitive package," as he dubbed it, using psychological jargon, quite simply as "hope." He has defined this view of hope as "Mental Willpower + Waypower for Goals." Translated into plain English, Snyder's definition of hope is a combination of a person's desire to achieve a certain goal plus his or her capacity for thinking through a variety of different ways to overcome obstacles along the route.[10]

Snyder wondered if hope, given this definition, could be defined quantitatively. Somewhat to his own surprise, he discovered that there was a workable way of measuring hope, the so-called Hope Scale. He also learned that the scale was a more accurate predictor of student exam success than some other more traditional systems of testing.[11] During research with some 3,920 college students at the University of Kansas, for example, Snyder found out that how a student scored on the Hope Scale was a more accurate predictor of the student's college grades than S.A.T. scores or the grade point average the student attained in high school.

Snyder explains: "Students with high hope set themselves higher goals and know how to work to attain them. When you compare students of equivalent intellectual aptitude and past academic achievements, what sets them apart is hope." He elaborates:

We are inherently goal-oriented as we think about our futures. In the words of the noted psychotherapist Alfred Adler, "We cannot think, feel, will, or act without the perception of a goal." Indeed, goals capture our attentions from the time we awaken in the morning until the time we go to sleep (where, should we dream, goals still appear in our minds). This conclusion holds whether you live in a Western or an Eastern culture, or any other for that matter. It is simply unthinkable not to think about goals.[12]

But can people invariably think through a solution to the jam they are in, as Snyder suggests elsewhere? Snyder's formula for hope, "Mental Willpower + Waypower for Goals," surely works in a large number of instances, especially for low-level or medium-level challenges where one of his almost whimsical aphorisms—"When the going gets tough, the hopeful keep going"—might well apply.

But what about those dark moments in our lives when tragedies and grief seem to crowd in upon us like vultures? Does a Hope Scale have simple answers for these occasions?

IN SEARCH OF PERSONAL HOPE

When I first began work on this book, this was one of several questions in my mind, but it was not there in any urgent way. I was a successful foreign correspondent working for a major national news magazine, back in Washington, D.C., for a few years after spending two action-filled decades overseas. My wife, two daughters, and I lived in a comfortable house in a leafy northern Virginian suburb. I was an active member of one of the largest and most missions-minded Episcopal churches in the United States. I enjoyed accepting invitations to speak to both Christian and secular groups across the country on issues relating to journalism and to the Christian faith.

I had always been intrigued by hope, but in something of a relaxed, almost detached manner. I had no concept of it as the *only* lifeline that at times can keep a person afloat when floodwaters of trouble and catastrophe seem certain to engulf him or her. But I learned how shallow my original notions had been when truly Jobian circumstances engulfed me over a period of two years. I also learned that hope is one of the most powerfully life-enhancing elements in all of human existence.

It was actually within months of beginning serious work on the book that the first waves of adversity began crashing upon the shore of my hitherto comfortable life. The first structure to give way was my marriage. From the beginning, the relationship my dear wife and I shared had been volatile and filled with stress. One obvious reason was that we were from different ethnic, national, cultural, and even social backgrounds.

H*opelessness is at the top of the list of cognitive patterns that underlie depression. The depressed person envisions a future filled with inescapable pain.*

Overseas, the close community of Christian friends and the novelty of each new place we lived in had somehow kept both of our heads just above water. But the normal turbulence and stress of marriage seemed to be exaggerated rather than quieted by the deceptive ordinariness of life in the American suburbs. Stress and tension reached a crescendo just about the time I was mapping out research for *Hope*. It seemed the only way we could provide a breathing space for both ourselves and our children was to separate physically.

How pathetic can you be? I asked myself. *You who have spoken so often of Christ's healing power and the victory in his blood? Here you are adding yourself to the sad statistical saga of marriage breakdown in the late twentieth century.*

The apparently irremediable breakdown of my marriage relationship was cataclysm enough. But the raw wound of this woe was made more stinging by great difficulties in the lives of my two lovely daughters, who were then entering their teenage years. Both were traumatically affected by the parental breakup.

There were financial difficulties: the need to sell our family home, depart from our wonderful, supportive neighbors and rural tranquillity in order to provide for two separate residences. As the sorrows kept piling up, I thought at times that I might have by now paid my dues to misfortune and could anticipate a lessening of the adversities.

But it did not happen. With our house on the market and only a thin membrane of civility somehow separating all of my family from total disintegration, my mother was suddenly diagnosed with a mortal illness in my native England. Her health went rapidly downhill, and within a few short months she died.

By now struggling to come to grips with *Hope* (the book), I realized there was nothing remotely academic anymore about my search for hope (the reality). If hope were not real, it would be quite hypocritical for me to write a book about it as though it were. I knew hope would not bring my mother back from the grave, but it must surely offer me more than a drunkard's condolence for the collapse of so much else in my life.

C ould the hope that had intrigued me as a book subject also be a quality that could bring light into the darkness of my own griefs?

I began to dig deep, not just into the substance of this book, but into faith itself and the connection of faith to hope. It seemed to me that now, more than ever, I had to answer a profound question: Could the hope that had intrigued me as a book subject also be a quality that could bring light into the darkness of my own griefs?

In the process, I came to grasp just why there is so much talk of hope in the New Testament. If you look through a concordance, you find it everywhere. Yet we know for a fact that most of the disciples were martyred for their faith, and the early church suffered relentless persecution from both religious and secular authorities. Despite this, they seemed to have a palpable sense of victory in their lives. It was obviously related to hope. What, I needed urgently to know, was this hope that Christians through the centuries have talked about? What was this hope that I so keenly needed myself?

I began the search in one place where it seemed there must be some clues: the Hebrew Bible. The ancient Hebrews talked relentlessly of hope, and few nations on earth seemed to have experienced so many national cataclysms as Israel had. Perhaps the Old Testament had some answers.

TWO

The Revolution
of Judaism

We who live under the comforting certainties of Judeo-Christian civilization have grown so complacent about those truths—which even now are increasingly being questioned in our own society—that we can scarcely grasp the revolution in philosophy and human values that occurred with the appearance of the Jewish faith centuries ago.

All ancient religions and cults had some system of morality and law. Some of the ethical and legal codes promulgated before the giving of the Jewish Law to Moses around 1250 B.C. deserve our admiration. The Code of Hammurabi (1792-1750 B.C.), for example, written during the reign of that Babylonian monarch, deals with family law, civil law, criminal law, and principles of economic life. It was, for its day, a remarkable attempt to establish fairness and social order within one of the earliest truly sophisticated civilizations of the ancient Near East.

ANCIENT GODS AND GODDESSES

But the Babylonians, for all of their brilliance, were confined within a religious cosmos populated by deities who were often chaotically at odds with each other. Nature, unpredictable and always dangerous, needed constant propitiating. But who, among the array of squabbling deities, was really responsible for it?

Life itself was short, unpredictable, often violent. Just when a civilization was becoming used to a particular pantheon of gods and goddesses, new conquerors would sweep in with new deities. Even though men and women were deeply superstitious about life and zealous to placate the unseen powers who alone seemed to understand the rules of life, harvest, disease, and death, they were often openly cynical about the relative power of each other's deities.

The historical books of the Bible illustrate this phenomenon vividly. The Second Book of Kings records the powerful King Sennacherib of Babylon (705-681 B.C.) sneering at King Hezekiah of Judah for daring to hope the Jewish deity would save Jerusalem from the Babylonian troops who had surrounded it. "Did the gods of the nations that were destroyed by my forefathers deliver them: the gods of Gozan, Haran, Rezeph, and the people of Eden who were in Tel Assar?" he asks in 2 Kings 19:12.

On an earlier occasion, officials of the King of Aram (approximately covering today's Syria) tried to explain that the reason for his failure to defeat King Ahab of Israel was that Israel's "gods" were gods of the hills rather than of the plains (1 Kgs 20:23). In effect, he was saying that they were more powerful on their own turf than the Aramean deities.

Cynicism and faithlessness will ultimately bring about the downfall of all nations and civilizations. They strangle the transmission to future generations of the spiritual ideas that animated its cultural and political achievements. Thus, even though monuments of stone remain to mark the existence and location of great powers of the past, very little else will survive.

Who today can speak of "the Babylonian tradition," for example, or "Aramean skepticism," or "Philistine jurisprudence"? No one, unless as a form of academic shorthand among specialists in the ancient Near East. Yet whether today one is a complete atheist or the follower of some non-Christian and non-Jewish faith system, it is impossible to deny the revolutionary impact of the Jewish tradition on the entire history of humanity.

A HERITAGE OF HOPE

What was it—and is it—that sent the great empires of the ancient Near East, despite the achievements of their monumental art and architecture, into history's great shredder while somehow enabling the Jewish tradition to flourish down to our own day? The answer has everything to do with hope.

To attempt to explain Judaism adequately as a system of thought and ideas in just one chapter would challenge the skills even of scholars who had spent a lifetime studying the subject. Yet there is broad consensus that Judaism instituted a complete revolution in thought about God.

It was not, in fact, the astounding notion that there was perhaps just one god: intimations of this were occurring contemporaneously with the emerging religious self-consciousness of the ancient Hebrews. The revolution introduced by Judaism was its utterly radical idea of the *character* of God: infinite, yet personal, revealing his heart to humankind, yet utterly separate in his holiness, omnipotent and demanding uncompromising allegiance among men and women, yet merciful beyond comprehension to human weakness and disobedience.

JEHOVAH—UNLIKE ANY OTHER

"What made the Jews different," says Denis Praeger, who is himself Jewish and a brilliant writer and public speaker on the subject of the biblical worldview, "was that they came into history and said, 'Stop!'"[1] Above all, says Praeger, the Jewish understanding of God was that he was utterly different from humankind. He was transcendent. He was also all-powerful, all-knowing, and totally righteous.

The traditional gods and goddesses of the ancient Near East all reflected, in the personalities attributed to them, the foibles and vices of human nature. But in the Hebrew Bible (the Old Testament) the word for goddess doesn't even exist. Jehovah is of such obviously different moral substance from other deities in the Bible, it is as if he were from a different universe altogether. And that, precisely, is the point.

This radical view of the nature of God's character colors absolutely every aspect of Judaism. Jewish morality, as promulgated through Moses on Mount Sinai, was absolute and universal in application. There were no exceptions. As one writer on Judaism, Leo Baech, explains, "The God of the Hebrews is neither Fate nor the World. He is exalted above them, because He is the just and holy One."[2]

Yet Jews believe, as Christians do, that this same God who revealed himself to the patriarchs Abraham, Isaac, and Jacob and then with great detail to Moses, is also a personal God. Though he is absolute in his demands upon us, he is also angered by our rebellion, grieved by our sufferings, and moved to action by our praise and our petitions. He is stern against immorality, yet merciful to those who repent of it. He is like a Father to all those who worship him and put their trust in him, and like a father, he delights in the obedience and the joys of his children.

HOPE OF ALL NATIONS

The sheer personalness of God strikes every observer of the Hebrew Bible. Leo Baech, for example, citing Psalm 63:1—"O God, you are my God, earnestly I seek you; my soul thirsts for you... in a dry and weary land where there is no water"—elaborates: "To man God is protection and help, a refuge and strength, hope and consolation, light and health, shepherd and keeper, the merciful one and redeemer." Hebrew piety, he says, has sounded the most intimate depths of the human heart.... At all periods He was the personal God to whom man could pray and speak.[3]

The characteristic feature of the Hebrew religion has always been the personal, living God, to whom people can come with their longings and their love, their tears and their praises, their fears and their hopes. This concept of God's personhood, inseparable from his perfection and his holiness, constitute, the second truly radical contribution of the Jewish faith to world civilization.

The third contribution, often overlooked in today's world, is Judaism's universalism. As we noted earlier, the deities of the ancient Near East all tended to be attached to particular localities or tribes, and often were thought to be powerless outside of these contexts. Yet Judaism asserts that Yahweh is not only the God of the Jews but the God of all nations.

The prophet Jeremiah is specifically told by God that he is to be a prophet to the nations (Jer 1:5, 10). One of the most striking aspects of God's covenant with the Jews in the Hebrew Bible is that God's calling upon the Jews is part of his larger plan to bring all nations under his sovereignty. "Through your offspring all nations on earth will be blessed," the Lord told Abraham (Gn 26:4).

King David's fame is such that, we are told in 1 Chronicles 14:17, "the Lord made all the nations fear him." King David himself, as the psalmist, later declares: "Proclaim among the nations what he has done" (Ps 9:11). With Judaism, says Baech, "an entirely new formative principle appeared among mankind."[4]

As Jews and Christians both understand it, this principle was nothing less than a revelation of the divine will for the whole human race. Jews themselves have seen this as a call "to form a new humanity and the future," as Baech puts it. Judaism, he says, "aims at a new world. This imperative that comes from the Beyond, this great contradiction of the world as it is, is one that seeks the ear of the whole world."[5]

AN UNFOLDING REVELATION

From the comfortable, at times even complacent perspective of a Christianity that has been culturally triumphant in the West for most of the past two thousand years, Christians today may overlook how radical this notion of divine revelation was. For one thing, it was an unfolding revelation. It was rooted in the historical events of the Jewish past, yet it looked unflinchingly into the future. No other religion before Judaism, and no religion after Christianity, has laid claim to the unfolding of future history with such breathtaking self-confidence.

In fact, the great revolutionary dynamic within the Judeo-Christian tradition is not so much a set of moral absolutes that both Christians and Jews believe were revealed by (the same) God, but a conviction that the

The revolution introduced by Judaism was its utterly radical idea of the character of God: infinite, yet personal, revealing his heart to humankind.

God who disclosed his thoughts, his laws, and his ultimate plans to the human race would remain in charge of history until the very end of time.

Scholar Milton Steinberg writes of what he calls "the triple hope" of Judaism: the expectation by the Jewish people of their ultimate deliverance and vindication; the hope that the individual soul will survive; the hope that society, in the end, will be regenerated into something fairer than its current form. Another way of defining the Jewish hope is the concept of God's "kingdom," his order of things both in people's personal lives and in the entire global society. "Touch Judaism where you will," says Steinberg, "and you will come across this concept of the kingdom, this dream of a perfected world peopled by regenerated men."[6]

Outside of Judaism in the ancient Near East, as Steinberg observes, men and women expected that "at best what had been would be forevermore, if indeed they were not persuaded of the more melancholy notion that the world was running steadily downhill from a Gold Age distant in the past and forever irretrievable."

Steinberg's reference is to the widespread belief among the Greeks, the

Sumerians, the Chinese, and others that the human race had once indeed lived in a condition that could be described as paradise. The ancient Hebrews, of course, knew of the Garden of Eden, a very brief transitional period between Creation and the Fall before mankind's real history began. But they focused far more upon a paradise yet to be. "The revolution was all the greater," notes Steinberg, "because, with time, the hope of the Kingdom overflowed not only Judaism and the Jews but all churches and creeds, to become in the end the common property and inspiration of all men of good will, whether devout or irreligious."[7]

THE MESSIANIC HOPE

Steinberg, of course, may have overlooked some of the problems caused specifically by the "irreligious" who took hold of the idea of a coming kingdom but separated it from the ethical obligations explicit in Jewish, and later Christian, beliefs. As we shall see in a later chapter, the concept of a utopia that men and women could create out of their own imaginations and abilities became, after the Renaissance, one of the most destructive of all the false hopes that humans have chased throughout history.

The Jewish vision of God's kingdom is often called the Messianic hope. Orthodox and conservative Jews have always believed that the kingdom of God would literally be inaugurated by the Messiah, the omnipotent

Our hope is... that we may make the world a kingdom of God and that all the sons of men may be thine.

ruler who would establish God's rule physically on earth and vindicate all of God's promises to the Jews. He would rescue them politically, vindicate them theologically, and save them spiritually.

Today, philosophical modernism has created something of a divide among practicing Jews. Many members of Jewish reformed congregations, particularly in the U.S., believe that the term Messianic is descriptive more of the nature of God's kingdom than of the rule by a particular person. Explains Rabbi Chaim Asa of Temple Beth Tikvah (literally, "House of Hope"), a reformed congregation in Fullerton, California:

"The Messianic hope is that man will make the best of the human condition by overcoming evil in the world and bringing God's kingdom to earth."[8]

Yet mainstream Judaism before the modern era had a much more concrete idea of the Messianic era. Leo Baech has this to say:

> The idea of the future is usually called "Messianic," because it originated in the hope of a Messiah—i.e., an Anointed One, a descendant of David.... He is the man who is to come; in him the history of the future gains personal form and color. He will usher in a kingdom of fulfillment, a kingdom in which wickedness or destruction, dispute or war, finds no place, an era of peace and reconciliation, the time when "the earth will be full of the knowledge of the Lord as the waters cover the sea" (Is 11:9).[9]

"I BELIEVE WITH PERFECT FAITH..."

In a very real sense, the Messianic expectation is an apocalyptic one: its advent is anticipated as the climax to momentous events in the history not just of the Jews but of the world as a whole. For Jews, indeed, the theological concept of salvation itself is postponed to the Messianic future. This contrasts with the Christian conception of salvation following immediately upon faith and confession in the one whom Christians hold to be their Messiah, namely, Jesus of Nazareth.

After the traumatic experience for Jews of the desecration of the Temple in Jerusalem by Roman legionaries of Titus in A.D. 70, and the banning of Jews from Jerusalem thereafter by the Romans, eschatological expectations rose among Jews. There were numerous false Messiahs, and their frequent appearance and subsequent exposure as false sometimes led to disillusionment over how events really would unfold for Jews in the end times.

It nevertheless remains an extraordinary feature of Jewish history that the Messianic hope keeps breaking forth through major Jewish teachers from age to age, despite repeated persecutions, setbacks, and disillusionment. Rabbi Moses ben Maimon, better known as Maimonides (1135-1204), philosopher, jurist, physician, and the foremost Jewish intellectual of the Middle Ages, defined thirteen doctrinal truths about Judaism that later found their place in Jewish prayer books. The last two of the items are ringingly Messianic:

> I believe with perfect faith in the coming of the Messiah, and though he tarry, I will patiently await his speedy appearance.
>
> I believe with perfect faith that there will be a resurrection of the dead at the time when it shall please the Creator, blessed be his name, and exalted be the remembrance of him for ever and ever.[10]

This reflects a vital part of the Jewish faith in post-Old Testament times, and the Jewish hope grew out of it as an expression of unfulfilled national spiritual longing in the Hebrew New Year prayer: "Our hope is... that we may make the world a kingdom of God and that all the sons of men may be thine."

For reformed Rabbi Asa, whom we met a little earlier in this chapter, there is still no assurance of a place in the Messianic future, however hard one tries, though "there is always hope." On the other hand, for conservative Rabbi Osrael Kelemer, of Congregation Mogen David in West Los Angeles, the Hebrew New Year prayer is quite literally "an expression of the Messianic hope."[11]

HOPE IN ATONEMENT

How did Jews find any real solace in hope in the traditional sense amid the perils and stress of life in the Diaspora? Interestingly, hope became deeply spiritualized within the concept of atonement from sin. Explains Rabbi Kelemer: "Atonement is a tremendous concept—God's gift to us. It is the reason for all hope.... The compassion of God—this is our hope. We are hopeless without this season of atonement."[12]

The *Talmudic Sayings of the Fathers*, in fact, sternly warns Jews against ethical behavior motivated solely by hope of reward. "Be like servants who serve without hope of reward," warns the sayings. "Let the fear of God in heaven be upon you." Hope nevertheless can maintain a toehold within Jewish ethics in the expectation that a good act performed will bear good fruit and will indeed, as part of the laws of the universe, "bring a blessing to him who accomplishes it," as Leo Baech explains. He elaborates:

> In this hope of reward, there is expressed the religious yearning of the soul, the tension between that which is and that which should be, and between that which is given to man and that which is promised to him.

"Those who sow in tears will reap with songs of joy" (Ps 126:5) is a truly human hope. For though we are to be pious for the sake of our lives, who does not also want to live happily in this piety?[13]

THE FOOTSTEPS OF MESSIAH

For most Jews today, however, the more narrowly conceived idea of hope as part of a moral life is still overshadowed by the great dimensions of the Messianic hope. Says Rabbi Kelemer:

The Messianic hope is primarily for the Jews as a people. It will be the age of the Messiah, but there will be an individual [actual person] Messiah. Today, we now hear the footsteps of Messiah. We are restored to our land. When is he coming? He has a big shoe size so we hear him at a distance, but it will be soon. We are in the throes of his appearing.[14]

By no means do all Jews have their faith and their hope set, as confidently as Maimonides and Rabbi Kelemer, on the personal advent of the Messiah. In fact, the unspeakable evil of the Holocaust still casts its shadow half a century after it took place. And as anti-Semitism, astonishingly, raises its ugly head once more in those European countries where it led to such murder and destruction, many Jews are pessimistic. Says Rabbi Asa:

Yes, pessimism has set in. Jews are far more skeptical about the good in man. It wasn't just the participation of the world in the Holocaust, it was the acquiescence in it. The nature of man is now in question. Goodness is not innate. It must be cultivated and nurtured. Parents must teach children to be good. As for the Holocaust, the world is moving more quickly. It has happened more than once, and it appears that it will happen again. Jews think of survival more than hope.[15]

Not all do. Rabbi Kelemer, for one, disagrees. "No," he argues, "the Holocaust did not destroy our hope, but it left a lot of questions. Some Jews turned against religion, and there was a lot of bitterness. In most of us, faith and hope remain. We don't understand, we accept."[16]

"Accept"—a Jobian response, surely, as in "The Lord gave and the Lord has taken away; may the name of the Lord be praised" (Jb 1:21). But in the Old Testament, the Jewish hope, while entirely Messianic, is also an affirmation not merely of God's promise to send the Messiah sometime in the future, but of God's profoundly reliable character right now.

THREE

The Old Testament Hope

The Bible is nothing if not the salutary story of a people who, though favored by God's special attention and love to a degree unique in human history, nevertheless succumbed again and again to the temptation to be disobedient, to worship other deities, and to forget the one who called them into being as a nation. Tragically, indeed, Jewish history in the post-Old Testament period is an almost nonstop account of nationhood suppressed, then restored, then suppressed again, before it was finally destroyed for nearly two thousand years.

Particularly in the post-exilic period, after A.D. 135, there is a wistful element of longing in Jewish spiritual thought that looks forward, not only to the earthly redemption of the Jewish nation through a return to the promised land, but to the final, Messianic redemption. The Passover and Rosh Hashanah (the Jewish New Year) in particular have been times when prayers were said in longing for better days both for individual Jewish families and the nation as a whole. For all Jews during the long exile centuries, "Next year in Jerusalem" became the epitome of yearning for national vindication.

PEOPLE OF HOPE

It is striking, therefore, that when that vindication finally came, during and after the long struggle to create the state of Israel, both secular and religious Jews agreed that the national anthem which would embody their deepest aspirations as a people would be "Hatikva," Hebrew for "the hope." The words had been composed at the very beginning of the modern Zionist movement at the end of the nineteenth century, and captured the universal longing of all diaspora Jews to return to their historic homeland.

The selection of a song named "Hatikva" was profoundly appropriate. There are ninety-five occurrences of the English word hope in some verbal or substantival form or other in the New International Version translation of the Old Testament. (There are 110 occurrences in the King James Version.) *Tiqwah*—to give the ancient Hebrew word its modern transliterated form—is translated to the English noun "hope" more often than any other Hebrew word in the Bible. *Tiqwah* is found thirty-two times in the Old Testament, and every time except for one, it is translated as hope. The one exception is when it occurs twice in the same sentence: "When she saw her hope unfulfilled, her expectation gone..." (Ez 19:5).

In Hebrew the word has an even more positive tone than in English, standing almost invariably by itself, concrete and graspable. "You will be secure," one of Job's companions, Zophar the Naamathite, assures his suffering friend, "because there is hope [tikwah]; you will look about you and take your rest in safety" (Jb 11:18). Nevertheless, Job is not consoled.

Eight chapters later he laments, "He tears me down on every side till I am gone; he uproots my hope [tiqwah] like a tree" (Jb 19:10).

It would be almost impossible in everyday speech to say "My hope is cut off" without immediately eliciting the follow-up question, "Hope of what?" As we saw in the first chapter, though there are many times when people say "There is really hope now," it is always in a particular context: hope for recovery from illness, of promotion in a job, of passing an important exam, of winning the love of someone very dear.

If a colleague walked into your place of work and announced, "There really is hope," depending on his previous reputation, you'd think he was either out to lunch or about to tell a cynical joke about the boss, the Post Office, or the Internal Revenue Service. In common English speech today, people just don't talk about plain old vanilla hope.

HOPE FOR EVERY LIVING THING

The ancient Hebrews knew better. The Old Testament, whenever it deploys the word *tiqwah*, insistently speaks of hope itself as something solid and meaningful, and not only to those who, like Job, have known success. In the Old Testament, absolutely everybody, and pretty nearly every living thing, can possess hope. The poor have hope (see Job 5:16), the afflicted have it (see Psalm 9:18), and even a tree has it, Job says in his argument with his friends (see Job 14:7). Hope is also something so universal to the human spirit that, during their lifetimes, even bad people naturally hold on to it.

"When a wicked man dies," King Solomon assures us (Prv 11:7), "his hope [*tiqwah*] perishes; all he expected from his power comes to nothing." We also learn from the same chapter that the hope [*tiqwah*] of the wicked ends "only in wrath" (11:23). "For what hope [*tiqwah*] has the Godless," Job himself asks, "when he is cut off, when God takes away his life?" (Jb 27:8).

This is interesting. Hope (*tiqwah*) is universal, common to the experience of good and bad people alike. Yet we learn that there is a different fate for the hope of the wicked from that of righteous people. How so? The answer becomes clear if the pattern of hope (*tiqwah*) is followed all the way through the Old Testament, and it is given most eloquently in the Psalms.

In the psalmists' poetry we discover that hope (*tiqwah*) comes, quite simply, from God himself. "Find rest, O my soul, in God alone; my hope [*tiqwah*] comes from him" (Ps 62:5). Nine psalms later, the psalmist is even more specific. "For you," he says, addressing the Lord, "have been my hope [*tiqwah*], O Sovereign Lord, my confidence since my youth" (Ps 71:5).

HOPE FROM THE LORD HIMSELF

This Old Testament usage of *hope* is something so precious to people, whether they are good or bad, that it sustains them in adversity when absolutely nothing else is available. Its extraordinary power to uphold is premised on one thing: it derives from the Lord himself. Moreover, we learn that we can be confident that this hope (*tiqwah*) will never be taken away from us as long as we are truly obedient to God in our lives. "Do not let your heart envy sinners, but always be zealous for the fear of the Lord," King Solomon advises his followers. "There is surely a future hope (not *tiqwah* here) for you, and your hope (*tiqwah*) will not be cut off" (Prv 23:18).

The interesting thing about this passage is that the Hebrew word translated as "future hope" is not *tiqwah* but *ahriyt,* which the Amplified Bible translates as "latter end" (a future and a reward), and this is a good paraphrase of what the word *ahriyt* actually means. Elsewhere, this word, which occurs sixty-one times in the Bible, is employed to indicate a person's final destiny, the ultimate outcome of a situation, even the possible eventuality of still undetermined circumstances.

> "*For I know the plans I have for you,*"
> *declares the Lord, "plans to prosper you*
> *and not to harm you, plans to give you a hope*
> *and a future.*"

King Solomon uses both *tiqwah* and *ahriyt* in exactly the same manner as the prophet Jeremiah hundreds of years later, when he announces the immensely comforting promise of God to the exiles from Jerusalem, whom King Nebuchadnezzar had taken away in captivity to Babylon. "'For I know the plans I have for you,' declares the Lord," Jeremiah writes in his letter, "'plans to prosper you and not to harm you, plans to give you hope [*tiqwah*] and a future [*ahriyt*]'" (Jer 29:11).

Two chapters later the Lord, through Jeremiah, makes the promise even more specific. "'So there is hope [*tiqwah*] for your future [*ahriyt*],' declares the Lord. 'Your children will return to their own land'" (Jer 31:17). Nothing Jeremiah could have said, speaking the words of God himself, could have given greater joy or more eager expectations to the exiled Jews than the assurance that they would return to their homeland from exile.

A PROMISED NEW COVENANT

At this moment—at the point of absolute reassurance during the time of their deepest despondency—Jeremiah speaks out to the Jews about something of far greater importance to them, and to the whole of humankind, than even their return from hated exile. Just a few verses down in the same chapter, God promises through his prophet a momentous new relationship with him, nothing less than "a new covenant with the house of Israel and with the house of Judah" (Jer 31:31).

This covenant is utterly unlike the earlier one sealed in fire and smoke through Moses on Mount Sinai.

Under the new covenant God tells the Jews through Jeremiah, "I will put my law in their minds and write it on their hearts. I will be their God, and they will be my people" (Jer 31:33). This seems clearly to be a Messianic prophecy. Christians themselves have interpreted Jeremiah's words as an Old Testament promise of the coming New Testament (or new covenant). Jeremiah, prophetically, appears to be looking forward to a time when forgiveness of sins comes to men and women independently of their performance of the Jewish law, when God will make his presence known in people's lives through something that, from the New Testament onward, came to be known as grace.

Tiqwah, to sum up, is positive, intuitive, and concrete. For Job, it is not absurd to ascribe the possession of *tiqwah* to a tree. For the psalmist, God alone is the source of *tiqwah*, and God is himself *tiqwah*. For Jeremiah, *tiqwah* and *ahriyt* are inseparable in God's blessings upon his chosen people from an even greater hope for their future: a new, unique relationship with God.

This hope (*tiqwah*) requires neither faith nor even effort to acquire: it simply is. The ancient Hebrews would have great difficulty comprehending the English expression "keep up your hopes" if it were translated literally into Hebrew employing the word *tiqwah*. It would make as much sense to them as saying, "Do not hope for bad things."

HOPE AS A VERB

But *hope* when used as a verb in the Old Testament (including forms such as *hopes* and *hoped*) is a different—and a revealing—story. The most frequently used verbal form of *hope* has no etymological connection with *tiqwah*. In fact, the word only acquires its connotation of expectation in English when it is employed in a very specific verbal context, and with an object, as in "hope in."

This is the verb *yahal*, which occurs forty-five times in the Hebrew Scriptures, fourteen of them with the direct translation "hope" in the verbal form, and seven of them with the translation "hope in." Perhaps one of the most dramatic illustrations of its meaning is found in Job's long reply to his false comforter friend Zophar. Desolate in his sufferings and depressed because of the inability of his friends to provide him with an adequate explanation of them, the most famous sufferer in the ancient world bursts out, "Though he slay me, yet will I hope in him," which the King James Version of the Bible translates as, "Though he slay me, yet will I trust in him" (Jb 13:15).

> There is surely a future hope for you, and your hope will not be cut off.

This expression is one of utter dependence and confidence, a confidence that does not require any understanding of what is happening. It might, of course, be translated as "to have faith in," but the implication is that, with the trust, there is an implied relationship with the person being waited upon. In fact, every time *yahal* is used except one, where *yahal* is translated as "put hope in" or "hope in," the one looked to is God, and the context is one of expectation that he will respond to this repository of hope in time of trouble.

"May your unfailing love rest upon us, O Lord, even as we put our hope in you," we read in Psalm 33.

"Why are you downcast, O my soul?" the psalmist asks repeatedly. "Why so disturbed within me? Put your hope in God, for I will yet praise him, my Savior and my God" (Ps 42:5; 42:11; 43:5).

Later, the ringing passages from Psalm 119 not only declare how much hope the psalmist has placed in God but what the consequences are among others who see it: "Do not snatch the word of truth from my mouth, for I have put my hope in your laws" (v. 43).

"Remember your word to your servant, for you have given me hope" [literally "made me to hope in you"] (v. 49).

"May they who fear you rejoice when they see me, for I have put my hope in your word" (v. 74).

"My soul faints with longing for your salvation, for I have put my hope in your word" (v. 81).

"You are my refuge and my shield; I have put my hope in your word" (v. 114).

In all of these Scriptures, the Hebrew verb translated as "put hope in" is *yahal*. It is instructive, moreover, that on the occasions where *yahal* is translated as "wait," as it is seven times, the word *hope* could as easily—and in some respects more illuminatingly—be substituted for it. Thus we have in Psalm 38, "I wait for you, O Lord; you will answer, O Lord my God."

HOPE FOR THE FUTURE

The third prominent and recurrent Hebrew word translated in the Old Testament as some verbal expression of hope is *qawahl*, which occurs in the Hebrew text forty-seven times. In seventeen of those occurrences, it is translated as "hope," either directly, as in "those who hope in the Lord will inherit the land" (Ps 37:9), or indirectly, as in "the caravans of Tema look for water, those traveling merchants of Sheba look in hope" (Jb 6:19).

At first glance the meaning of *qawahl* seems hardly distinguishable from *yahal*, i.e., to put one's hope or trust in someone or something: "No one whose hope is in you will ever be put to shame," says Psalm 25, "but they will surely be put to shame who are treacherous and without excuse." Other examples of this meaning of *qawahl* are frequent:

"May integrity and uprightness protect me, because my hope is in you" (Ps 25:21).

"Even youths grow tired and weary, and young men stumble and fall, but those who hope in the Lord will renew their strength" (Is 40:30-31).

"Do any of the worthless idols of the nations bring rain? Do the skies themselves send down showers? No, it is you, O Lord our God. Therefore our hope is in you, for you are the one who does all this" (Jer 14:22).

But it is clear from other contexts that *qawahl* contains a connotation of future time. In the twelve cases where *qawahl* is translated as "wait" or "wait for" when referring to God, there is an element of expecting something to happen in the future, something that God himself will sometimes be involved in. Thus in Psalm 40, we come across "I waited patiently for the Lord; he turned to me and heard my cry."

In Lamentations, there is even a sense of waiting with malicious glee for something unpleasant to happen to someone else. "All your enemies open their mouths wide against you," the prophet warns his people; "they scoff and gnash their teeth and say, 'We have swallowed her up. This is the day we have waited for; we have lived to see it'" (Lam 2:16).

There is another occurrence of the word *qawahl* in Job, this time signifying waiting as a tedious and highly stressful matter. "May its morning stars become dark," Job groans out in cursing the day of his birth, "may it wait for daylight in vain and not see the first rays of dawn, for it did not shut the doors of the womb on me to hide trouble from my eyes" (Jb 3:9-10). We are no longer in the rarefied air of waiting upon and trusting in the Lord with hope in our hearts. *Qawahl* shows us the anguish that lies in wait for us when hope is malicious or bitterly disappointed.

"LET NOT MY HOPES BE DASHED"

There are just two other Hebrew words that deserve our attention because the English translators of the Hebrew Bible have chosen *hope* to convey their meaning. One is the verbal form *sabar* and the other is its derived noun form, *seber*.

Sabar is translated variously as "hope," "to look," or "to wait," while *seber* is rendered simply "hope." *Sabar/seber* lacks the concrete and deeply positive sense of *tiqwah,* the sense of implicit trust of *yahal,* or the connotation of something coming up, not necessarily for your good, of *qawahl.* In *sabar/seber* too, there is the possibility of a malign hope.

In Esther, for example, we learn that, on the holiday later to be celebrated by Jews as Purim, "the enemies of the Jews had hoped to overpower them, but now the tables were turned and the Jews got the upper hand over those who hated them" (Est 9:1).

There can be an element of uncertainty about the outcome of hope in *sabar/seber*, as we see in Psalm 119: "Sustain me according to your promise and I will live; do not let my hopes be dashed." But it, too, can denote the abiding belief in God's reliability and his faithfulness to remain with us under all circumstances.

"Blessed is he whose help is the God of Jacob," says the psalmist in that rambunctious outburst of praise in the last seven psalms, "whose hope is in the Lord his God, the maker of heaven and earth, the sea, and everything in them—the Lord, who remains faithful forever" (Ps 146:5). More philosophically, the author of Ecclesiastes comments on why it is important to be active as long as one is alive, "for the grave cannot praise you, death cannot sing your praise; those who go down to the pit cannot hope for your faithfulness" (Is 38:18).

There is a sense of dependency in this usage of *hope;* when we look at the other occurrences of *saber/seber* combination, it is confirmed with a startling image when the translation is "to look to." Now we see the Bible referring to the utter dependency of men and women upon God for the most basic needs of life. In fact, *sabar* and *seber* are used interchangeably in relationship with human beings and the entire animal world. "These all," says the psalmist, having just referred with a sweep of his hand to all of the creatures in the oceans, "look to you to give them their food at the proper time" (Ps 104:27).

Fifty psalms later, we find that people also must have that same relationship to God of "looking to," very much in hope. "The eyes of all look to you," the psalmist states unequivocally—presumably including good and bad people, "and you give them their food at the proper time" (Ps 145:15).

When the sense of *saber/seber* is "wait," there is similarly an idea of expectancy without any time frame—a hope that is totally dependent on circumstances that are out of one's control. In Psalm 119, where hope in God's word is stated again and again, the psalmist quietly asserts in a moment of subdued and reverential praise, "I wait for your salvation, O Lord, and I follow your commands" (Ps 119:166).

HOPE IN THE ALMIGHTY

We conclude our search for the essence of Old Testament hope with an intriguing Hebrew word that is found only five times in the Hebrew Bible, and yet on each occasion is translated as *hope*. This is *miqwehl*. The interesting thing about this word is that its rare usage has a special quality that is different from that of any of the other Hebrew terms translated as hope. In essence, *miqwehl* is the collective hope of the Jewish people, none other than the Almighty himself.

We first come across *miqwehl* when King David, with that unique ability to humble himself before the Lord and to exult in the Lord's presence at the same time, is dedicating the gifts for the building of the Temple that his son Solomon will complete. "But who am I, and who are my people, that we should be able to give as generously as this?" he asks (1 Chr 29:14). "We are aliens and strangers in your sight, as were all our forefathers. Our days on earth are like a shadow, without hope" (v. 15).

This seems a modest beginning for *miqwehl*. Why didn't King David say "without *tiqwah*"? The answer is first hinted at in the next occurrence, in Ezra 10, when the Jews who have just returned from exile in Babylon are weeping before the Lord. Ezra himself has just wept bitter tears over the marriages that many of the Jewish men contracted in exile with non-Jews, and his own public contrition convicts the hearts of all of the returned exiles.

Just then, however, Shecaniah, a prominent returnee, pipes up. "We have been unfaithful to our God by marrying foreign women from the peoples around us," he says in confirmation of Ezra's own words. Then he adds, "But in spite of this, there is still hope for Israel" (Ezr 10:2). He too, like King David, obviously has something very concrete in mind, yet it is not *tiqwah*.

> *Why are you downcast, O my soul? Why so disturbed within me? Put your hope in God, for I will yet praise him, my Savior and my God.*

Miqwehl in some ways gives a more momentous meaning to hope than any other Hebrew word used for it. The word is nothing less than an attribute of God himself. It is the prophet Jeremiah who makes this clear. "O Hope of Israel," he implores in a prayer of great distress after describing the punishment of famine and the sword that God is about to unleash upon unfaithful Judah, "its Savior in times of distress, why are you like a stranger in the land, like a traveler who stays only a night?" (Jer 14:8).

Two chapters later, Jeremiah has seen the first glimmerings of an answer to his prayer. But again, this "hope" is part of the very attribute of the Almighty: "O Lord, the hope of Israel, all who forsake you will be put to shame. Those who turn away from you will be written in the dust because they have forsaken the Lord, the spring of living water" (17:13).

THE HOPE OF THE FATHERS

Finally, in the last occurrence of *miqwehl* in the Bible, we learn that the "hope of Israel," whom the people of Judah had temporarily abandoned, will not only rescue them but will punish the people he had originally used to judge them for their sins. The tables will now be turned. The only reason they had suffered in the first place, Jeremiah assures his people, attributing this remark to their enemies, is that "they sinned against the Lord, their true pasture, the Lord, the hope of their fathers" (Jer 50:7).

We have, chronologically and symbolically, moved from a vivid, generic hope—*tiqwah*—that was the common possession of all the Jewish people and even, by extension, of the trees of the field, to the real hope of Israel,

God himself. It is almost as if the repeatedly tragic history of the Jews, in the Old Testament relationship of themselves with God, prepared them for a hope that was not simply solid and vivid but would last forever.

Tiqwah
Hope from God himself

Ahriyt
Hope for a latter end, a future and a reward

Yahal
To hope, or to put hope in

Qawahl
To wait in expectation, to hope for the future

Sabar/Seber
Hope, dependent on circumstances out of one's control

Miqwehl
Collective hope of the Jewish people, the Almighty himself

FOUR

Hope in
Other Faiths

"Faith," says the famous opening passage at the beginning of the eleventh chapter of the Epistle to the Hebrews, "is being sure of what we hope for and certain of what we do not see" (Heb 11:1). Faith is at the center of all religions in some form or other. To be committed to a particular religious worldview or way of life requires a belief in the efficacy of that religion to bring solace, reward, or perhaps simply the avoidance of punishment for unbelief.

Contrary to the assumptions of many people today, faith does not have to be blind, though in some instances it indeed may be, nor does it require a mealy-mouthed false humility to be truly sincere. In fact, every living person today requires at least some measure of faith to perform the most trivial of life's daily demands.

A MEASURE OF EVERYDAY FAITH

You get up in the morning and turn on the shower. Based on experience, the expectation is that hot or cold water will come out. But there is never an absolute guarantee that it will. What if the water heater has broken down, or there is a drought in progress, or even more infuriating, you forgot to pay your water bill and the authorities turned the water off altogether?

You get in a car to drive to work and you turn the key in the ignition. Do you have to pray each day that the engine will start? (Well, some of us have at times owned cars so ornery that a veritable exorcism has seemed necessary to get them to work, but that's another story.) Even if people do pray for their engines to catch when they fire the ignition, they certainly exercised some faith in the quality of the automobile when they laid down money to buy it.

Later in the day, you are likely to exercise quite a lot of faith about human performance. You need faith on a really cold morning in January that the school bus will show up when it's supposed to, or that your car pool to work won't have a collective case of the flu. You may have to dig up some faith that the check you are about to deposit (or perhaps the one you yourself have just written) won't bounce, that the repair man will come Wednesday morning as he promised and not Thursday afternoon, or that the boss won't go back on his word to give you a raise if you complete an important assignment ahead of schedule.

These are descriptions of common or garden-variety faith. This faith is not something philosophers or theologians spend much time thinking about, but it's pretty essential not just to your own life but to civilization itself. And there are plenty of higher levels of it: starting your own business, boarding a commercial jet the day after a tragic crash involving the same airline, or starting a friendship or romance.

In fact, all modern technological civilizations require a surprising amount of faith in both the reliability of people (Did the pilot go to bed early enough to be wide awake for this early morning takeoff?) and equipment (Does the plane's radar system really work?) and, implicitly, the workmanship and maintenance that enables equipment to keep on working with virtually no attention.

LACKING A HOPEFUL VISION

When it comes to the faiths of different religions, there are huge differences between those faiths that are linked to the quality of hope and those that are not. It might be argued that the central ingredient that enables various religious civilizations not just to survive but to flourish, to renew themselves and adapt vigorously to changing circumstances, is not the intensity of faith in their presuppositions but whether they contain the essential ingredient of hope.

Any faith system, any civilizational structure that either lacks or loses hope may not necessarily die out. On the other hand, it is unlikely to cope successfully with secular modernity or with the challenges of other more hope-oriented faiths. What is striking about many of the major world religious systems other than Judaism or Christianity is the extent to which they lack a hopeful vision of the world and the future. Perhaps that is why Christianity is making greater inroads into these faith systems than the other way around.

It is important to say at the outset that this is not intended as a judgment of disrespect for such religions. Devout Hindus and Buddhists can and do make claims that their faith offers the best approach to dealing with life's challenges or explaining its complexities. What they would surely have difficulty doing is claiming that the power of hope is an important ingredient in the mainstream of their faiths.[1]

THE NOTION OF KARMA

Both Hinduism and Buddhism are India-originated religions that contain the notion of *karma*. This term, thanks to the fascination of the American youth counterculture of the 1960s with eastern religions, has effectively entered the English language (as in several Hollywood movies where a character, encountering setbacks in some situation or other, mutters, "It must be bad karma"). Karma is the doctrine that what happens to a person in his or her present life is the product of good or bad decisions made in a previous physical incarnation.

This, in turn, presupposes another core Hindu doctrine, the transmigration of one's soul from birth to rebirth in a potentially endless chain of physical existences. Explains one authority, "The law of karma assumes that every deliberate action has its own consequence and pursues the doer, often beyond the grave."[2]

Karma is the doctrine that what happens to a person in his or her present life is the product of good or bad decisions made in a previous physical incarnation.

Karma can thus be a daunting inhibition to any idea of hope at all. As another authoritative and nonhostile source observes:

This belief [karma] is indissolubly connected with the traditional Indian views of society and earthly life. It has given rise to an acquiescence that may verge upon fatalism—the belief that any misfortune is the effect of karman [sic], of one's deeds, and so one's own doing.... Such doctrines also encourage the view that mundane life is not true existence (the so-called Indian pessimism) and that human life ought to be directed toward a permanent interruption of the mechanism of karman and transmigration.[3]

Juan Mascaro, the brilliant translator of the great Hindu classic writings known as the *Upanishads,* has this to say:

> The law of evolution called Karma explains the apparent injustice in the world with sublime simplicity. There is a law of cause and effect in the moral world. We are the builders of our own destiny, and the results are not limited to one life, since our Spirit that was never born and will never die must come again and take to itself a body, that the lower self may have the reward of its works. Good shall lead to good, and evil to evil.[4]

THE HINDU GOSPEL

But it does not need to be left to commentators upon Hinduism, least of all foreign ones, however sympathetic they may be to the Hindu cosmology, to confirm this point of view. The most well known of all Hindu classics is the *Bhagavad-Gita,* "the Gospel, one may say, of India," according to a famous Western admirer, Aldous Huxley.[5] In the *Bhagavad-Gita,* the Hindu deity Krishna himself acknowledges the centrality of karma. "I established the four castes," he tells the warrior Arjuna in the pre-battle conversation that comprises the setting of the religious classic, "which correspond to the different types of guna and karma. I am their author; nevertheless, you must realize that I am beyond action and changeless."[6] In the *Upanishads,* in the section entitled "The Supreme Teaching," it is said of karma:

> According as a man acts and walks in the path of life, so he becomes. He that does good becomes good; he that does evil becomes evil. By pure actions he becomes pure; by evil actions he becomes evil. And they say in truth that a man is made of desire. As his desire is, so is his faith. As his faith is, so are his works. As his works are, so he becomes.[7]

The problem with this worldview is that the cycle is potentially endless. How to escape it? In the same section of this Upanishad, a clue is offered:

> He who is free from desire, whose desire finds fulfillment, since the Spirit is his desire, the powers of life leave him not. He becomes one with Brahman, the Spirit, and enters into the Spirit.... When a man

sees the Atman, the Self in Him, God himself, the Lord of what was and of what shall be, he fears no more.[8]

Brahman and Atman are concepts that are central to Hinduism. As we shall see, taking a close look at them makes it clear why Hinduism has indeed led to the impression of widespread fatalism among devout Hindus and why, more importantly, whatever cultural refinements Hinduism may have achieved over the years, this faith of 751 million adherents has almost nothing to say about hope.

THE "ALL-EMBRACING PRINCIPLE"

Hinduism, it is almost a cliché to say, has defied every attempt at definition, and is perhaps less concerned about metaphysical clarification than any other great religion. But from its evolution as the system of worship of the Indo-European peoples who settled in northern India in the last centuries of the second millennium B.C., it has nonetheless held to a core of key beliefs to which virtually all Hindus subscribe, whatever their various idiosyncrasies about local deities and practices.

Aside from the concept of karma, Samsara, the process of rebirths, and the authority of the caste system and the ancient Vedic texts, the most important concept is that of *Brahman-Atman.*

Brahman has been described as "the belief in an uncreated, eternal, infinite, transcendent, and all-embracing principle, the ultimate reality of all life,"[9] "the single, central fact" of Hindu cosmology.[10]

> B*rahman… is the belief in an uncreated, eternal, infinite, transcendent, and all-embracing principle, the ultimate reality of life.*

Brahman is what is sometimes called "Godhead," an abstract entity that constitutes the final irreducible quality of all things without the personal attributes of God as evident in Judaism or Christianity. It is the concept that lends Hinduism its pantheistic character: God, in effect, is both *in* everything and *is* everything.

Now Atman is the self in all living things, yet it is also a part of Brahman. This is why Hindus who have spent some time in the West will often say, to the perplexity of their Western audiences, "We are all part of

God." Huxley enthusiastically endorses this view in his own introduction to the *Bhagavad-Gita*.

In every human being, he claims, there is "the spark of divinity," and by identifying ourselves with this spark we can come to an intuitive knowledge of Brahman. "The Hindus," he asserts, "categorically affirm that thou art That—that the indwelling Atman is the same as the Brahman."[11]

Juan Mascaro makes it even more explicit: "The central vision of the *Upanishads* is Brahman, and although Brahman is beyond thoughts and words, he can be felt by each one of us as Atman, as our own being."[12] But in pointing this out, Mascaro perhaps unwittingly reminds us of one of the key points that radically separates Hinduism from Christianity.

HINDUISM VERSUS CHRISTIANITY

First, in Hinduism God is not personal. Second, he is not separate from us. Even Huxley, who mistakenly asserts that "in regard to man's final end, all the higher religions are in complete agreement,"[13] acknowledges that orthodox Christian belief disavows any identity between a so-called spark of divinity in ordinary humans (i.e., the Atman) and God himself.[14]

Yet Mascaro makes it clear that the great classics of Hinduism un-

> A *tman is the self in all living things, yet it is also a part of Brahman.*

equivocally assert that man and God are of identical substance. "Thus the momentous statement is made in the *Upanishads*," he writes, "that God must not be sought as something far away, separate from us, but rather as the very inmost of us, as the higher Self in us above the limitations of our little self."[15]

Numerous passages from the *Upanishads* make it luminously clear that this is indeed a central view of Hinduism. The *Svetasvatara Upanishad* states, "God is in truth the whole universe: what was, what is, and what beyond shall ever be."[16] Similarly, from the *Maitri Upanishad:*

Samsara, the transmigration of life, takes place in one's own mind.[17]...
Even as water becomes one with water, fire with fire, and air with air,
so the mind becomes one with the Infinite Mind and thus attains final
freedom.[18]

Then, from the *Chandogya Upanishad:*

There is a Spirit which is pure and which is beyond old age and death
and beyond hunger and thirst and sorrow. This is Atman, the Spirit in
man. All the desires of this Spirit are Truth. It is this Spirit that we must
find and know: man must find his own Soul. He who has found and
knows his Soul has found all the worlds, has achieved all his desires.[19]

Some contemporary Hindu practitioners in the West have taken this
concept to the point of asserting godlike freedom of action for themselves
first, and then for their followers. Thus Rajneesh, who operated a
religious center in Oregon for several years, told his red-clad devotees: "I
am going to destroy you utterly. Only then can I help you,"[20] and, "As
you are, you are God."[21] The emotional, psychological, and social dangers
implicit in this teaching hardly need to be belabored to be grasped.

HINDUISM AND HOPE

There is a more fundamental point. If, after all, we ourselves are part of
God and yet cannot bootstrap ourselves up to what Aldous Huxley calls
"the ultimate Unity of the Divine Ground [i.e., the Brahman],"[22] not to
mention improving our karmic condition through countless future
reincarnations, what is left for us to hope for?

For the vast majority of people who are neither gurus nor full-time
professional meditators, it is no consolation at all to rest one's hope of
health, happiness, or a sense of purpose on the very faculties of mind and
body that have already proved to be inadequate for this task. Hope itself,
in the Hindu cosmology, is interpreted merely as "desire," and desire is
viewed as a negative, destructive force that makes true spiritual enlightenment impossible to attain. From the Hindu point of view, desire leads to
both a physical and a spiritual dead end.

The Hindu deity Krishna makes this explicit in his conversation with the warrior Arjuna in the *Bhagavad-Gita*. Musing on the tragic folly of engaging in a battle in which he will be compelled to kill members of his own family, he asks Krishna, who is the incarnation of the Hindu deity Vishnu:

> What can we hope from
> This killing of kinsmen?...
>
> Krishna, hearing
> The prayers of all men,
> Tell me how can
> We hope to be happy
> Slaying the sons
> Of Dhritarastra [a rival king]?[23]

He goes on: "Krishna, how can one identify a man who is firmly established and absorbed in Brahman? In what manner does an illumined soul speak? How does he sit? How does he walk?"[24]

THE CONCEPT OF DETACHMENT

Krishna's reply is remarkably similar to the attitude of the Stoic philosophers of Greek and Roman antiquity. Here is Marcus Aurelius: "Keep yourself simple, good, pure, serious, free from affectation, strenuous in all right acts."[25]

And here is Krishna: "Do your duty always," he exhorts, "but without attachment. This is how man reaches the ultimate Truth; by working without anxiety about results."[26]

Any form of positive expectation is to be rejected, Krishna warns: "Stop hoping for earthly reward. Fix your mind on the Atman. Be free from the sense of ego."[27]

From an ethical point of view, it is not unreasonable advice. However, from the perspective of the search of men and women of all ages and conditions for a meaning to their own lives and a hope for something better than what they live with in both the circumstantial and the moral sense, Krishna's counsel offers no hope at all.

It is hardly surprising the only inroads that Hinduism has made in the West, therefore, have been among young people already rendered empty by the nihilism of a post-Christian culture. Later on, we shall see how Westernized Hinduism, and indeed Buddhism, established a foothold in

Western culture originally through the medium (perhaps literally as well as figuratively) of a virulently anti-Christian theosophist who had studied the occult arts in Tibet—Helena Blavatsky.

BUDDHISM CONTRASTED WITH HINDUISM

Buddhism, though established in India where Hinduism held sway, differs from Hinduism in some important ways. First, it is truly a global religion, with devout followers spread across the globe in large numbers from Tibet to Japan, from Mongolia to Vietnam.

Second, it is one of only two world religions, the other being Christianity, whose name is derived from an attribute of its founder. *Buddha* means "Enlightened One," the name given to Gautama (563-483 B.C.). Christ, of course, derives from *Khristos*, Greek for "Anointed One," or Messiah.

The late Christmas Humphreys, an English courtroom lawyer and later a judge, was a devout Buddhist and an internationally respected expositor of his faith. Yet he demonstrated as much ignorance of Christianity as zeal for his own religion when he asserted: "To the extent that Buddhism is true it is, like the essence of Christianity, beyond the accidents of time and place, of fact and history."[28]

Third, though Buddhism adopted much of the cosmology of Hinduism in India, it acquired from the varied cultures where it took root a unique variety of forms of the faith. In fact, the term faith may only legitimately be applied to a handful of Buddhist schools, most notably the Hodo School of Japan, mentioned in an earlier footnote.

As Christmas Humphreys put it, "By the usual tests [Buddhism] is not a religion so much as a spiritual philosophy whose attitude to life is as cool and objective as that of a modern scientist."[29] Indeed, "to the Buddhists, all weight and emphasis is on the mind, and none on the circumstance," declares a famous Buddhist sutra (scripture).[30]

The point is a significant one, for Buddhists cannot even agree among themselves over the extent to which their religion is theistic. According to Humphreys, "As between the theist and the atheist positions, Buddhist is atheist."[31] But according to one of the greatest Western scholars of Buddhism of the past century, Edward Conze, "If atheism is the denial of the existence of a God, it would be quite misleading to describe Buddhism as atheistic."[32]

A PHILOSOPHY OF SUFFERING

What Buddhists do agree upon is that Buddhism is to a large extent a philosophy of suffering. Buddha's Four Noble Truths are the omnipresence of suffering; its cause, which is wrongly directed desire; its cure, the removal of desire; and the noble eightfold path of self-development, which leads to the end of suffering.[33]

Buddhas's Four Noble Truths

- The omnipresence of suffering;
- Its cause, which is wrongly directed desire;
- Its cure, the removal of desire;
- The noble eightfold path of self-development, which leads to the end of suffering.

"To the Buddhist," as Humphreys puts it, "good and evil are relative and not absolute terms. The cause of evil is man's inordinate desire for self. All action directed to selfish, separative ends is evil; all which tends to union is good."[34] Buddhists regard belief in the very existence of self to be "an indispensable condition to the emergence of suffering."[35]

Yet Buddhist cosmology does not allow for any simple way out. Since Buddhism accepts the laws of karma inherited from Hinduism, one who does not escape from the relentless cycle of unhappy incarnations is "predestined by the previous exercise of [his] own free will" to be bound to the permanent "Wheel of Becoming," as Humphreys puts it.[36]

The universe in Buddhism is constantly evolving; nothing is permanent—everything is in a process of transformation. There is no cause, rest, or finality in Buddhism, no forgiveness of one's sins, not even the ultimate darkness of death itself, for though everything dies, life itself in a deeper sense is indivisible.[37]

IN SEARCH OF DHARMA

The entire aim of Buddhism is to seek *dharma,* a word that can be variously translated as "truth," "ultimate reality," "righteousness," or *Nirvana,* a term that "encapsulates the very highest state to which a Buddhist can aspire." Almost lyrically, Conze says of Nirvana that "we are told that Nirvana is permanent, stable, imperishable, immovable, ageless, deathless, unborn, and unbecome, that it is power, bliss, and happiness, the secure refuge, the shelter, and the place of unassailable safety."[38]

One who attains this state will be exempt from return to the cycle of reincarnated and karmic suffering. In a sense, Nirvana and dharma constitute the ultimate hope of Buddhism, a hope to end all other hopes. The only difficulty is, how does a person reach them?

It becomes apparent early on in any study of Buddhism that achieving dharma is a task that may require literally several separate (reincarnated) lifetimes. It is considered virtually impossible for an ordinary layperson (a "householder," in the common translation of the term from Buddhist scriptures) to attain it unless he either spends the remainder of his life until death within a monastic order or has had the good fortune to have been a monk in several previous existences.[39]

The importance of the monastic life for Buddhism is evident in every country where Buddhism is

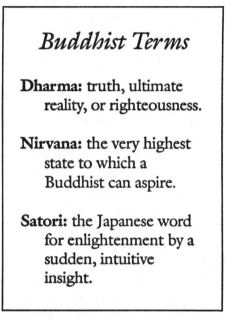

Buddhist Terms

Dharma: truth, ultimate reality, or righteousness.

Nirvana: the very highest state to which a Buddhist can aspire.

Satori: the Japanese word for enlightenment by a sudden, intuitive insight.

still a strong faith among ordinary people. Monks are the "Buddhist elite," in Conze's words, and the life of a householder is "almost incompatible with the higher levels of spiritual life."[40] Even for a monk, moreover, it is in meditation alone that Buddhists believe is to be found the chief means of salvation[41] and even then, the notion of salvation is vastly different from that in Christianity.

Ananda Coomaraswamy, a prominent twentieth-century Hindu writer, acknowledges the element of fatalism in Buddhism. He explains: "The karmic law merely asserts that this direction [of the present course of events] cannot be altered suddenly by the forgiveness of sins, but must be changed by our own efforts."[42]

Conze admits, somewhat defensively, that the insistence of Buddhism upon the doctrine of "not-self" (*an-atman* in Sanskrit) "has earned for Buddhism the reputation of being a 'pessimistic' faith."[43]

Humphreys goes further. Formulating during his studies of Buddhism "Twelve Principles of Buddhism" that he says virtually all Buddhist schools accept as foundational to their religion—for Buddhism has no formal creed—he includes an assertion of nonpessimism as his twelfth principle. He states, "Buddhism is neither pessimistic nor 'escapist,' nor does it deny the existence of God or soul, though it places its own meaning on these terms."[44]

For his part, Conze justifies the extraordinary strenuousness of the Buddhist's search for happiness on the grounds that modern psychology and philosophy have empirically demonstrated that human beings are in general unhappy, and that anxiety itself is central to "the core of our being."[45]

A QUEST FOR ENLIGHTENMENT

Meditation is a lonely discipline at the best of times, but the Buddhist who embarks upon it in his or her search for Enlightenment will get no outside help. Another of Humphreys' "Twelve Principles" is number eleven, a quotation from Buddha himself: "Work out your own salvation with diligence."[46] The sheer relentlessness of the task of finding any hope in Buddhism has led the faith into some surprising—and occasionally sinister—byways.

Zen Buddhism, which developed in Japan, is an effort to pass behind the intellect altogether and achieve *satori. Satori* is the Japanese word for enlightenment by a sudden, intuitive insight that Zen students believe can be attained by the sudden confrontation of the mind with a paradoxical idea. The Zen school developed several *koans,* or riddles, the best known of which has become a sort of cliché of trendy contemporary American writing: "What is the sound of one hand clapping?" Contemplating these *koans* is said to help students of Zen break free from the bondage of ordinary logic and help their minds achieve *satori.*

What Humphreys admits as "the hunger of Buddhist hearts for a heavenly city" has also led to the cult of a future Buddhist Messianic figure, the Maitreya, who will appear on earth countless millennia after the original Buddha. This Maitreya will lead the human race into a true paradise even though the original Buddha's teachings may by that time have been completely forgotten.[47]

THE DARK SIDE OF BUDDHISM

Inevitably, though, the very permissiveness of Buddhism has led to its corruption in some of its expressions by ugly demonolatry, sorcery, and shamanism. Nowhere is this truer than in Tibetan Buddhism, where dark supernatural forces, derived from preexisting forms of demonic worship that prevailed prior to the advent of Buddhism in Tibet, are routinely conjured up for purposes that often seem to have nothing to do with the individual's quest for enlightenment or escape from the wheel of Samsara.

As Conze uneasily acknowledges, "Nowhere save in Tibet is there so much sorcery, and 'black' magic, such degradation of mind to selfish, evil ends, and much of these men and their practices has been described by travelers."[48]

It does not seem to have occurred to Conze that to rest humanity's desire to escape from the cycle of human suffering on human effort alone creates a sense of deep powerlessness. And whether those efforts are made in meditation or in righteous action, they are certain to reinforce the very sense of helplessness that led to the search in the first place. That, in turn, may be only one logical step away from a plunge, for some people, into the blackest alleyways of the supernatural in the search for personal power.

In one of the innumerable Buddhist scriptures attributed to Buddha's teaching through the words of humans, angels, and even animals, an unpretentious cuckoo makes it clear, representing Buddha in conversation with other birds, that the possession of hope can actually be a hindrance on the spiritual journey. "To hope for miraculous blessings, and still have wrong opinions—that prolongs the bondage," the precociously self-confident bird asserts at one point. "To try to understand one's inner mind while still chained to hopes and fears—that prolongs the bondage."[49]

Buddhism has no sure hope at all to offer its adherents, either in this life or the probably multitudinous—and uncertain—lives that humans are doomed through karmic destiny to experience in the future. As one observer has noted:

> The only salvational element in Buddhism is the prospect of salvation from rebirth. Whereas the Christian West takes a positive view of being in the world, Buddhism sees the highest value in non-being.... Thus it is not merely a tragic conception of the world that distinguishes

Buddhism from Western religions, but the position of man in relation to natural processes, and the question of how he is to deal with the tragic aspect of these processes.[50]

Dharma may thus constitute an admission that hope, in and of itself, is not an admissible aspiration for the human race.

MOHAMMED AND THE KORAN

Islam doesn't go as far as Buddhism in questioning the value of hope when contemplating the ultimate issues of life. For the true follower of the faith, Islam assures many wondrous rewards in the believers' paradise. What it leaves open, however, is who, in the end, will gain access to that paradise. In fact, only one category of Muslim, one who is a martyr for the faith—whether in a jihad (holy war) or as a victim of persecution—is totally assured of all the ultimate rewards of the true believer.

Islam means "submission." When the founder of the faith, Mohammed (A.D. 570-632), first responded to what Muslims believe was a call from God to "recite" the Koran, he did so in the belief that he himself was a submitted one (i.e., a "Muslim"). Throughout his life, Mohammed struggled with both the sense of compulsion under which he acted to proclaim the new faith, and the frustration and anger that he was not accepted as a prophet of God by the two faith groups whose approval he most eagerly sought, namely Jews and Christians.

Mohammed claimed to be both the rightful and final heir of the Jewish prophetic tradition and its Messianic successor, Christianity.

Five Pillars of the Muslim faith

- The profession of faith— "There is no God but Allah and Mohammed is His prophet."
- Fasting during the month of Ramadan
- Alms to the poor
- Prayer five times a day facing Mecca
- The pilgrimage, haji, at least once in a believer's lifetime, to Mecca itself

In his identification with the Jewish tradition, the first direction of the Islamic *qibla* was toward Jerusalem; it was only when the Jews emphatically rejected his claim to be a prophet in the tradition of the patriarch Abraham and the lawgiver Moses that he turned the *qibla*—the Muslim direction of prayer—toward Mecca, the most holy city in the Islamic faith. As for the Christians, his attitude toward them was ambivalent: not as hostile as toward the Jews, who resisted his theological position far more vehemently than the Arabian Christians of the day, but suspicious nonetheless.

Both Jews and Christians belong in the Islamic category of "People of the Book," a category lower than that of Muslims but higher than that of pagans who engage in open idolatry. Islam goes to great lengths to dispute the Christian assertion that Jesus physically died on the cross and was then resurrected by God from the dead. And the Koran itself argues that Jesus was taken up to heaven and replaced on the cross by someone else at the last minute.

"ALLAH, THE COMPASSIONATE, THE MERCIFUL…"

In his penetrating and yet fundamentally sympathetic book *Islam,* the British Arabist Alfred Guillaume printed out the text of the Apostles' Creed, an early and foundational statement of Christian faith. By italicizing the words of the creed that Islam did not accept, Guillaume illustrated powerfully just how much of Christianity Islam has chosen to accept. In fact, almost exactly half—fifty-four—of the 109 words in the English version of the Apostles' Creed would be acceptable to Muslims.[51]

What is left out of the cosmos of Islam, however, is the very center of the Christian interpretation of God's attitude toward the human race: his totally sacrificial love. Islam speaks of Allah as "the compassionate, the merciful," and has many different names to denote his attributes. Love, however, is not among them.

In fact, as another sympathetic (and not at all explicitly Christian) observer has noted of Islam:

> Throughout the Koran, the principal motivation for accepting God and believing in His revelation appears to be fear: fear of the last judgment and fear of eternal damnation. Though God is described as generous

and beneficent, He is always the God who punishes unbelievers and destroys corrupt societies.[52]

In fact, the Koran explicitly states that it is God who inspires with both fear and hope, not necessarily with any consistent purpose. In Sura 13 (Thunder), the Koran declares: "It is He who makes the lightning flash upon you, inspiring you with fear and hope, as He gathers up the heavy clouds."[53]

The fear is made palpable in those fiery passages of the Koran in which the fate of unbelievers and those who reject the Prophet Mohammed is described. "For unbelievers," says Sura 17 (Man), "We have prepared fetters and chains, and a blazing Fire."[54]

In Sura 98 (The Proof), this is even more vehemently asserted: "The unbelievers among the People of the Book and the pagans shall burn for ever in the fire of Hell. They are the vilest of creatures."[55]

Clearly, not even Jews and Christians, although they are People of the Book, will escape from hell if they consciously reject Mohammed's claims to be a Messenger of God. In fact, Mohammed declared that God assured the Muslims that their Christian and Jewish opponents had already abandoned any hope of resisting the Islamic advance. Declares Sura 5 (The Table): "The unbelievers have this day abandoned all hope of vanquishing your religion. Have no fear of them: fear me."[56]

HOPE FOR ISLAM'S FAITHFUL

As for the faithful who are accepted by Allah into paradise, the promised rewards are rich. They will recline in a sensually delightful paradise on soft couches in robes of silk, attended by dark-eyed houris and good-looking young men, feeling neither cold nor heat.[57] The difficulty for all Muslims is always how to gain that acceptance.

The standard response of devout Muslims is that the pathway to righteousness is to fulfill the Five Pillars of the faith: the profession of faith—"There is no God but God and Mohammed is His prophet"; fasting during the month of Ramadan; alms to the poor; prayer five times a day facing Mecca; and the pilgrimage, haji, at least once in a believer's lifetime, to Mecca itself.

Even with devout adherence to these requirements by all Muslim believers, however, there is no certain hope of winning paradise. In Sura

24 (Light), reference is made to mosques in which "morning and evening His praise is sung by men whom neither trade nor profit can divert from remembering Him, from offering prayers, or from giving alms; who dread the day when men's hearts and eyes shall writhe with anguish; who hope that Allah will requite them for their noblest deeds and lavish His grace upon them. Allah gives without measure to whom He will."[58]

The clear meaning of this usage of hope, however, is "desire with no certainty of result." In fact, in Sura 19 (Mary), Mohammed's transmission of God's message is quite explicit—absolutely everyone will experience at least some measure of hell: "There is not one of you who shall not pass through the confines of Hell: such is the absolute decree of your Lord."[59]

Allah, to be sure, will deliver some from this torture soon enough, but "wrongdoers" will suffer permanent torments on their knees. Yet during his lifetime, not even Mohammed's closest family members had any assurance that they would indeed be rescued from hell quickly.

THE CHARACTER OF ALLAH

There are two reasons for this state of uncertainty about entry into the Islamic paradise. One is the character of God as Muslims describe him and as he appears in the Koran.

To emphasize God's awesome power and separateness from mankind—and perhaps to distinguish him even more decisively from the pagan deities of Mohammed's Arabia—the Koran repeatedly speaks of him as someone whose will cannot be determined—who can, if he chooses, be utterly capricious, and who reserves entirely for himself the reasons for accepting or rejecting those who would follow him.

"When the records of man's deeds are laid open and the heaven is stripped bare," proclaims Sura 81 (The Cessation), "when Hell burns fiercely and Paradise is brought near; then each soul shall know what it has done."[60]

ISLAMIC PREDESTINATION

The other reason for eternal uncertainty is the Islamic doctrine of predestination. The Koran in various places suggests that the fate of every person is sealed the moment he or she is born. Two examples: "Every misfortune that befalls the earth, or your own persons, is ordained before

We bring it into being" (Sura 57: Iron).[61]

"We have made all things according to a fixed decree. We command but once; Our will is done in the twinkling of an eye" (Sura 54: The Moon).[62]

"Islam," writes one scholar of comparative religion, "does not recognize the need for penitence in the Judeo-Christian sense. Nor do Moslems experience a real longing for salvation. Allah is irrational and unpredictable; the only tenable attitude for man is therefore total humility."[63] Even Muslims of the most nominal commitment to their faith will nevertheless say "Insha'allah," meaning "if God wills it," before making even the simplest statement of intention to do something in the future. "Insha'allah" is, for Moslems, a form of spiritual protection from inadvertently trespassing on God's very different planning.

One of Islam's appeals is nevertheless its assertion that all human beings are spiritually equal in the sight of Allah. Even though women have much lower status in the Islamic paradise, Islam declaration of the spiritual equality of all humanity gives the faith considerable power as a vehicle for massive social mobilization.

HOPE IN MARTYRDOM

Moreover, it is a characteristic of Islam that the one feat of Islamic devotion which assures entry into paradise, in the face of whatever other failings an individual might have, is to be a martyr in the cause of Islam. The very term *martyr,* in the Islamic sense, is strikingly different from the Christian understanding of the term. Several Islamic terrorists who have murdered countless others have earned the title "martyr" from their co-religionists when they died in the course of killing. By contrast, it is central to the Christian concept of martyrdom that the one being martyred either goes to death unresistingly or is killed for no reason other than his profession of faith.

For those Muslims who do not wish to engage in a jihad against the enemies of their religion, however, Islam offers no assurance at all that a follower of the faith has been righteous enough to escape a long time in hell once he or she is dead. A former Christian missionary to Iran during the time of the Shah recalls once meeting a group of pilgrims in that country on the way from Meshed to Nishapur, where the famous Persian poet Omar Khayyam and a revered Shi'a figure, the Imam Reza, are both buried.

"Now you are going home," the missionary inquired of his fellow travelers on foot, "are you sure that God has accepted your pilgrimage and forgiven your sins?"

"Oh no," the pilgrims replied, "only God knows that."[64]

AWAITING THE MAHDI

In the ultimate sense, of course, the pilgrim was correct: In all three major monotheistic faiths, only God ultimately knows all things. Yet in virtually every major religion and culture there is a yearning for personal assurance of spiritual worth that defies both legalism and the unwillingness of the religious authorities to make the doctrinal pronouncements usually necessary for that assurance.

The aspiration breaks through the surface of orthodox belief again and again, often erupting in spasms of fanatical allegiance to a new religious leader from within the faith. The newly emergent leader is invariably a charismatic individual with immense spiritual self-assurance. On his coattails of self-confidence, so to speak, others of the faith believe they will secure a more reliable ride into paradise, heaven, Nirvana, or whatever the state of immortal bliss may be.

Of the two main branches of Islam, the Sunni and the Shi'a, it has been in the Shi'a, the smaller of the two, that the messianic tradition has become not just strongly developed, but a significant part of the religious tradition. The most important Shi'a sect is that of the "Twelvers," so called because its followers believe that there have been twelve Imams (literally, "leaders") in the line of descent from Ali, the fourth Caliph of the Muslim faith, and Fatima, one of Mohammed's wives.

In the "Twelver" schema, the 13th Imam, Muhammad al-Madhi, disappeared from the world in A.D. 880 and has supposedly been hidden by God until his coming again as the Madhi, which literally means "guided one." "All of the various sects of the Shi'a have this hope in common," says Guillaume in his own treatment of the subject.[65]

It is virtually certain that the tradition of the Mahdi was influenced by the Christian doctrine of the Second Coming of Christ, even though, as Guillaume asserts, the phenomenon of belief in a future messianic leader appears to be common to several world cultures, including those of India, China, Peru, and Mongolia.[66] British imperial troops in the nineteenth century fought at least two colonial wars to suppress uprisings led by would-be local Mahdis.

By far the most serious was the revolt of the Mahdi in Sudan that was crushed by the British General Sir Herbert Kitchener at the Battle of Omdurman in 1898, with the young Winston Churchill galloping furiously against the foe in a famous cavalry charge. A large body of apocalyptic literature in Persian deals with speculation over the date of the return of the Mahdi, the redeemer of the faithful in the Shi'a worldview.

Sunni tradition holds, by contrast, that the Mahdi will play a crucial role at the end of the age in the destruction of the antichrist, a figure who has a place in Islamic eschatology. In his world-renowned introduction to the philosophy of history, the Muqaddimah, the Tunisian-born medieval Arab historian Ibn Khaldun (1332-1406) wrote in 1377:

> It has been accepted by all Muslims in every epoch, that at the end of time a man from the family (of the Prophet) will without fail make his appearance, one who will strengthen Islam and make justice triumph. Muslims will follow him, and he will gain domination over the Muslim realm. He will be called the Mahdi. Following him, the Antichrist will appear, together with all the subsequent signs of the Day of Judgment. After the Mahdi, Jesus will descend and kill the Antichrist. Or, Jesus will descend together with the Mahdi, and help him kill the Antichrist.[67]

Ibn Khaldun goes on to question the reliability of these traditions within Islam, but he does not dispute their currency.

THE RISE OF SUFISM

For many Muslims, however, even the tradition of the Mahdi who is to come has not satisfied the need for a sense of actual communion with God. Thus there arose the tradition of Sufism (the word is based on the Arabic word for wool, which the early Sufi adherents used to wear as a means of displaying their contempt for the comforts of the world), the Islamic mystical tradition. In many respects it was Sufis, rather than conventional Islamic prelates or laypeople, whose zeal contributed greatly to the missionary expansion of Islam, particularly in medieval times.

Sufis emerged as a vital element in the Islamic tradition in the second century after the establishment of the faith. Protesting the luxurious living and the decadence of the Caliphates of Damascus and Baghdad, they sought a closer relationship with God in asceticism, prayer, fasting, and religious exercises. To a striking degree though, the path they trod theologically had been walked upon before them by followers of the two main Indian religions we have already discussed. Their desire for union with God led them to monism, the belief that everything is God, and some of their number were executed for heresy in proclaiming ecstatically that they and God were one. To a degree that is strikingly reminiscent of Hinduism, the achievement of fana is the "extinction of the personality in the reality of the divine."[68]

One of the most famous of the Sufis, the Spanish Muslim philosopher Muhyi al-Din Ibn al-Arabi (d. 1240), took the position that there is no distinction at all between God and the world he made, but that in Mohammed was embodied a philosophical principle that combined in human form all of the mysteries of the universe. The notion comes close to the Christian doctrine of the Logos, the Word who became flesh (Christ).[69] Among other things, al-Arabi wrote:

> Thus man is both created accident and eternal principle, being created and immortal, the Word which defines and which comprehends. Through him, all things came to be; he is the bezel-stone of the signet ring, on which is inscribed the sign with which the King seals his treasures.[70]

It is now established also that al-Arabi, who first wrote an account of the infernal region, the heavens, and paradise, had an enormous influence on Dante before the Italian poet wrote *L'Inferno* or *Il Paradiso*.[71]

SEARCHING FOR SOMETHING TO HOPE FOR

There is some question as to how much the Islamic Sufis were influenced by the Christian mystical tradition, which was strong in Spain at the same time as Sufism itself flourished in the peninsula. On the other hand, Sufism may also have been simply responding to the fundamental human need, having once postulated the existence of either God or some ultimate divine principle, either to come as close as possible to him as the human personality will permit, or to seek the intermingling of the personality with the substance of God himself.

Clearly, though, whether in expectation of the Mahdi or in the mystical ecstasies of Sufism, large numbers of devout Muslims throughout Islamic history have not been satisfied with the cheerless spiritual future offered by orthodox Islam. They have, in effect, been searching for something to hope in and hope for, a consolation in the present and a promise for the future.

Their search, interestingly, has been continued into modern times by many who have dramatically rejected both Islam and any of the traditional global religions. In light of the palpable failure of so many of the ostentatiously nonreligious efforts to satisfy mankind's evident need for hope, particularly in our own century, we might not be expected to pay these efforts much attention. But even false hopes are sometimes accurate pointers to true ones.

FIVE

The Enlightenment and the Seeds of False Hope

I t would be a hard-hearted individual who looked without anguish at the almost desperate efforts of world religions over several millennia to satisfy the universal human need for salvation.

THE SEARCH FOR THE MEANING OF LIFE

If we don't call it "salvation," what do we call it? Security, a sense of purpose in life, assurance that there is something beyond death? Every civilization for which there are early written records shows from its beginnings an almost desperate effort to find out how to placate the gods, or if not gods (and goddesses), the unseen forces perpetually beyond humanity's control.

Even highly rational and well-organized civilizations such as ancient China or imperial Rome have found the need to resort to divination to answer the most perplexing questions of both public and private life. Christians, somewhat smugly at times, perhaps, have sometimes put it that there is a "God-shaped vacuum in the human heart" that yearns to be filled. But even agnostics would have to admit that the search for a meaning to life beyond the material evidence of the senses is one of the constant themes of human endeavor in all ages and throughout all cultures.

The great English Christian writer C.S. Lewis was convinced that, in the final conflict among world faiths, the contest for the affections of the human race would ultimately be between Hinduism and Christianity.

Hinduism, Lewis noted, absorbed all other systems within it, while Christianity excluded them.[1]

The explanation is simple enough: Hinduism claims to embrace within its arms all religious insights of all world religions. There are many truths, it says, and at the same time, they are all one (or One, as is often written to indicate that the "one" here has a divine quality to it). Christianity, by contrast, says quite explicitly that there is only one truth, since Jesus Christ himself embodies all truth.

Though challenged by the rise of Islam in the seventh and eighth centuries, the Christian faith so permeated the culture and thought of Europe for one-and-a-half millennia after the death of Christ that the Messianic hope became inextricably intertwined with the "common sense" understanding of hope that is common to all civilizations. It led to a cultural self-confidence, particularly after the Renaissance and the Reformation, that took European culture and the Christian faith to almost every corner of the globe within just three centuries after the discovery of the Americas by Columbus.

HISTORY INSPIRED BY HOPE

It is true, of course, that European exploration and expansionism from the early fifteenth century onward was propelled by a variety of motives, many of them selfish and greedy. A major factor in the voyages of discovery by the Portuguese down the coast of Africa, around the Cape of Good Hope, and then across the Indian Ocean, for example, was the desire to find a new route for the importation of valuable spices into Europe. Yet no honest appraisal of Christopher Columbus himself can deny a fervent faith element among all his other calculations of the dangers involved in an uncharted voyage across the Atlantic. As Archbishop of Canterbury George Carey put it:

It is no exaggeration to say that all human progress has been inspired by hope. Hope drove Christopher Columbus westwards and hope was the magnet which drew the early American settlers into the unconquered territories of the wild west. Hope continues to be the spring of human activity, sacred and secular. Man cannot live without hope.[2]

Hope, in the sense of a firm conviction of God's rulership over the universe, fueled the great upsurge of European science in the seventeenth and eighteenth centuries. Isaac Newton (1643-1727) was one of the greatest physicists of all time and the man who laid the foundations for all of theoretical physics until the advent of Einstein's relativity theories of the twentieth century. Newton was a devout Christian believer. He and virtually all the other major scientists of his day confidently explored the mysteries of the solar system, the fundamental properties of matter, and the structure of physical laws because they believed that God's laws were both immutable and knowable.

HISTORICAL LANDMARKS IN EUROPE

The enormous confidence inherent in this belief led to the astonishing scientific and technological progress evident during the Industrial Revolution of the late eighteenth century and to what may now be considered a virtual idolatry of science itself. By the mid-nineteenth century, the ability of science to uncover ever new areas of knowledge and solve certain material challenges of human life led some to believe that science alone would be sufficient to improve the entire human condition.

The scientific revolution in Europe drew its philosophical impetus from a faith in the consistency of God's laws and his will for mankind. Yet other major historical factors in European life helped propel it rapidly forward as well. First and most important among them was the Renaissance, which gave momentum to an explosion of intellectual curiosity about the world of both mankind and nature.

Second was the Reformation, which established the principle of justification by faith and personal accountability to God. Without such a powerful new sense of the importance of the individual in God's plan for the human race, the new social and political structures favoring scientific discovery might have taken much longer to come into being. From the Reformation's insistence on the "priesthood of all believers" arose a liberating conviction that God's blessings upon Christians no longer required priestly mediation.

The third important factor was the great breakthrough in religious tolerance and political freedom that accompanied the end of the religious wars in Europe (the Thirty Years War in particularl, 1618-1648), especially in England, the Glorious Revolution of 1688 in which the principle of parliamentary supremacy over the monarchy was established.

THE SEEDS OF FALSE HOPE

But the openness of human thought that these powerful developments brought to Europe also carried with them seeds of ideas that, within just two or three centuries, were to undermine the faith foundation that had made them possible in the first place. The Renaissance opened up European thought to the sunlight of Greek and Roman classicism in the field of painting, sculpture, and literature. But it also provided an entry point within European Christendom to occult and pagan ideas that had been all but driven from European culture since the pan-European triumph of the Christian faith by the end of the first millennium after Christ (with the obvious exception of Spain, under Arab Muslim rule from the seventh century to 1492).

The Renaissance, of course, hardly led to an upsurge in pagan idolatry of a classical Roman or even Dark Age Teutonic variety. But the intoxication of intellectual experimentation after centuries of often despotic control of thought by the institutionalized church had some ominous results. One of them was the emergence of a view that man himself, in the complexity of his physical and spiritual nature, was but a microcosm for the whole universe. This evolved into a conception that human life is inseparably connected with every other phenomenon in existence: monism, the belief that everything is one.

Nowhere was this outlook given greater welcome than in Italy, in Florence in particular, arguably the great incubation chamber of the entire Renaissance adventure. The most famous scholar of the Italian Renaissance, Giordano Bruno (1548-1600), a brilliant, witty, and acerbic thinker, developed a physical theory of the universe that proclaimed the unity of all matter. By contrast, the Aristotelian view, which had been the accepted view of the church in pre-Renaissance times (particularly as articulated by St. Thomas Aquinas), has always held that no entity can be both itself and something else at the same time. The common sense expression of this view is simply this: If an elephant is truly an elephant, it cannot at the same time be a giraffe. Yet the theory of the unity of all matter expresses at heart the Hindu view of life: all is indeed one.

"DIVINE ESSENCE"

Once monism shows up on the scene, pantheism is almost certainly just around the corner. Sure enough, other fifteenth and sixteenth-century Italian scholars in Florence, notably Pico della Mirandola (1483-1496), had already substituted for the traditional Christian view of creation a conception of the universe as an emanation from divine essence. Bruno's monism went further. He held that there was a basic unity of all substance and all opposites within a divine Being. This in turn led him to an elitist view that religion was something to guide the ignorant masses while philosophy was the possession of a select few, who were qualified both to master it and to rule.

Bruno, whose personal fate was tragic (he was handed over to the Inquisition by the Venetians and burned at the stake in Rome), had a profound impact upon subsequent intellectual and spiritual developments in Europe. So did an exceptionally talented Dutch Jew named Benedict de Spinoza (1632-1677), who believed that God was completely identical with the world and thus neither transcendent nor possessing any personality. From this position, Spinoza next concluded there could be no such thing as human free will since humanity was an integral part of the great unity of God-and-the-world.

The evolution of European philosophical thought in the seventeenth and eighteenth centuries is a complex story, and it is hardly possible even to begin to do it justice in just a few short paragraphs. Nevertheless, with the hindsight of three centuries, two threads stand out consistently in the overall design. Both of them—at times seeming to be woven in different directions, at times interweaving with each other—helped form a consistent intellectual and philosophical pattern whose function was to eclipse and then obscure altogether the Christian view of faith and hope.

One of those threads is European Rationalism, the broad philosophical movement to establish unaided human reason as the principal device for investigating the human condition (and thus implicitly rendering faith irrelevant to those judgments). Benedict de Spinoza, in one respect, belonged to this thread, which became historically prominent first in the mid- to late-eighteenth century in France (especially during the French Revolution of 1789), and second during a burst of atheistic polemics in England and Germany respectively during the 1840s and 1870s.

The second thread is usually named Idealism. Strictly speaking, it refers to much of German philosophy and theology during the early nineteenth century. But whereas Rationalism tried to shoulder Christianity aside by demonstrating, supposedly, the superiority of reason to faith, Idealism sought to co-opt Christian vocabulary and symbols to create a worldview in which the crucial Christian moral distinctions between Creator and creation, between good and evil, between the individual and the mass, no longer applied. In the end, Idealism opened the door to a "spiritual monism" that, for all intents and purposes, amounted to Hindu pantheism. But more of this in a moment.

THE ENTHRONEMENT OF REASON

Rationalism is a term that in post-Renaissance Europe had its origins in the ideas of Rene Descartes (1596-1650), who is frequently quoted, "I think, therefore I am." Descartes was a mathematician who sought to establish in the realm of philosophy the same rigorous logic that entranced him in the realm of mathematics. The emphasis, though, was on *a priori* thinking—drawing conclusions based solely on the internal laws of human logic, without regard to revelation or faith.

Descartes believed that it would be possible for men and women to agree upon philosophical principles, if lucidly enough devised, in a manner no different from their agreement on principles of, say, geometry. Philosophy, in effect, might have laws capable of discovery, if people would shine on them the "natural light" of reason.

But this natural light, if a consistent device of human thought, must also be applied to the assertions of revealed religion, and to Christianity in particular. In effect, from Descartes onward, the Rationalist tradition made reason the ultimate arbiter of truth. In principle, there was nothing intrinsically hostile to Christian belief in this position. After all, ever since the death of Christ, many highly "reasonable" people had come to the conclusion that the Christian faith was true.

Gradually, however, reason came to be synonymous with merely whatever was observable through the human senses. By the early eighteenth century, the Rationalist tradition had led to the phenomenon in England of Deism. Deism was a set of beliefs that generally asserted the existence of a Supreme Being, the need for repentance for sins, rewards and punishments in the next world. However, Deism specifically denied the particular truth of specific religious faith, Christian or any other.

English Deism, with its skeptical, indeed irreverent spirit, was influential in France in the first quarter of the eighteenth century. In fact, it became the badge of many of the philosophies of the French Enlightenment in the mid-century, even when, like [François Marie Arouet] de Voltaire, some of them ridiculed the church and orthodox Christian belief.

The French Deists borrowed ideas heavily from the English but were generally polite in expressing them. Voltaire himself, though lambasting the institutional Roman Catholic Church of his day, never thought to attack religious-based ethics. But other French philosophers, notably Denis Diderot (1713-1784), were far less restrained and deployed the methods of Rationalist argument to attack not just the church and its foibles, but Christian faith itself.

Diderot started his philosophical and literary journey by introducing to the French public the ideas of English Deist the third Earl of Shaftsbury. However, Diderot's *Pensees Philosophiques* (1746) were the beginning of a lifelong campaign to undermine Christian belief. Paradoxically, such assaults on Christianity, though they were through Diderot's disciples and successors to reach paroxysms of fury during the French Revolution, did not have lasting impact upon the role of Christian belief in French culture.

When Napoleon Bonaparte took over the helm of the French state in 1799, he needed spiritual respectability. Therefore, the atheistic radicalism of the revolutionaries was swept aside, not to reemerge in France for nearly a century. What struck the most powerful blow at the roots of the Christian faith in Europe were not the efforts of French philosophers, but of German theologians and Bible scholars.

For the French, predominantly Roman Catholic, disputes over biblical interpretation were not of great philosophical importance. After all, for Roman Catholics the ultimate authority for matters of faith and doctrine was the church, not the Bible itself. But for Germans, Christian authority was, quite simply, the Bible. Martin Luther had established in Germany the Reformation principle of the authority of God's Word over all other sources of Christian faith and practice. He had even provided the foremost German translation of the Bible, in circulation well into modern times.

ASSAULT UPON SCRIPTURE

The most damaging thing that could be done to the Christian faith in Germany was not to criticize the church, which was overwhelmingly Protestant in the north of the country, but to cut away at the roots of all Protestant Christian authority in the country—the Bible itself. From the middle of the eighteenth century onward, while the French were glorifying *la raison,* German scholars were building up their own Enlightenment with a frontal assault upon Scripture.

The Hamburg professor R.S. Reimarus (1694-1768) depicted Jesus as a ranting enthusiast put to death by the Romans for purely political reasons. This was later to be seen as the first shot fired in a crescendoing volley of assaults by German scholars on the veracity, plausibility, and above all allegedly supernatural elements of the Gospel records. As Albert Schweitzer, who closely followed the history of German theology, put it:

> The history of subsequent theology [from the late eighteenth century] is the history of the debates between those who have wanted to discount the supernatural and those who have insisted that it must be taken into consideration in any assessment of Christianity and the Biblical records.[3]

Schweitzer was understating the case: The impact of the German assault on the Bible was to reverberate well beyond mere theology into philosophy and political theory. In the end, it was to replace the Christian hope entirely with a totally secular view of the human race. In this view, all human aspirations were to be focused on changed structures of society rather than on changed individuals within society. In a nutshell, the German assault on biblical authority changed forever how people viewed the possibility of human progress.

While the French were glorifying la raison, *German scholars were building up their own Enlightenment with a frontal assault upon Scripture.*

French Rationalism, meanwhile, reached its logical apogee during the most brutal moment of the Revolution, the Terror of 1793. While the guillotines were frantically severing heads from bodies in Paris and other locations in France, a grand Festival of Reason was celebrated in October of that year in the most famous church building in the French capital, Notre Dame Cathedral. An actress, clothed in white drapery with a blue cloak over her shoulders, was carried into the church as a representation of the Goddess of Reason.[4] Reason and atheism thus briefly triumphed at the state level in France, but the very excesses of the revolution itself discredited its idolatrous extremes of Rationalism.

The German story was different. The relentless whittling away of the authority of the Bible had its most important consequence among German philosophers, who had at least originally paid lip service to Christian belief. The outstanding German Enlightenment philosopher Gottfried Wilhelm von Leibnitz (1646-1716), who had drunk deeply of the belief system of Spinoza in long conversations with the Dutch Jewish pantheist, in public downplayed his associations with the controversial philosopher.

However, by the time of Johann Wolfgang von Goethe (1731-1832), the outstanding figure of all German literature, skepticism toward the Christian faith was not only acceptable, it was fashionable. By the 1790s, there was also a revival of interest in the thought of Spinoza. One of those coincidences of history that seem, in retrospect, to portend great changes in thought or society, came in the year 1793. That was the year, of course, of France's revolutionary "Terror," which also saw the publication by the German Rationalist philosopher Immanuel Kant (1724-1804) of *Religion Within the Limits of Reason Alone.*

Kant was not just the foremost philosopher of the German Enlightenment but one of the most influential thinkers in modern Europe, and his book is filled with abusive references to Christianity. Worship of God within an institutionalized religion was "a religious delusion," he held, using an obscene term in the book itself.[5] Kant's most famous work, *A Critique of Pure Reason,* had already hacked away at the roots of religious belief so strenuously that one famous observer, the German poet Heinrich Heine, commented: "With the blade of his criticism, his *Critique of Pure Reason,* Kant, the executioner, beheaded belief in God. God, therefore, now became nothing but fiction."[6]

One of Kant's admirers was a young German scholar, Georg Wilhelm Friedrich Hegel, who at the time was delving into the origins of Christianity from a highly skeptical vantage point. What he was to come up with was not exactly hope but is the basis of most of the surrogate secular religions—with their surrogates of hope—that have dominated the twentieth century.

THE LEGACY OF HEGEL

Georg Wilhelm Friedrich Hegel (1770-1831) was one of the greatest philosophers of all time. It is impossible to understand the developments of European ideas, not to mention of the Nazi and Marxist ideologies of the twentieth century, without grasping at least something of his thought. His influence on Western thinking as a whole was so profound that nineteenth, and twentieth-century philosophy in Europe has been described by one observer as "a series of footnotes to Hegel."[7] Without Hegel, there would have been no Marxism—and no Leninism either—and the entire tragic history of Communist Party rule in the twentieth century might conceivably have been averted.

H*egel completely rejected the Christian faith—and its message of hope—as the basis for any effort to "restore" the human being.*

Ironically, there might not have been any Nazism either, for Hegel's thought in political terms lent itself, depending on who interpreted it, to two possible interpretations. "Right Hegelianism" held that whatever existed politically was exactly what should exist (i.e., Prussian authoritarianism as practiced in Hegel's day was just fine). "Left Hegelianism" held that history was calling for a qualitative change to the order of things currently in existence.

HEGEL, HOPE, AND PHILOSOPHY

What has Hegel got to do with hope? At one level, nothing, and at another, everything. To start with, the entire tone of Hegel's writing was deeply hostile both to the traditional Christian view of human life and to the Jews. When still in his twenties in the 1790s, Hegel wrote that the Jews were "corrupt" because they themselves had concocted the doctrine of the corruptness of human nature.[8]

Of the Christian faith in particular, he had this, among other things, to say: "To consider the resurrection of Jesus as an event is to adopt the outlook of the historian, and this has nothing to do with religion."[9] As we noticed when looking at the Baghavad Gita through the prism of Aldous Huxley, to remove the historical outlook from religious questions is to sever the connection between faith and truth.

This, of course, is precisely the position adopted by pantheists, for whom reality is always in the end subjective, and for whom the best that people can hope for about life in general is that either eventually they will manage to escape it or that somehow they will merge with it in a way that enables them to lose their separate individuality.

Hegel, as a gifted student of his life and work has said, "emphatically... was not a [Christian] believer" and was not in the least bothered by Kant's scathing disdain for Christianity. He compared Jesus unfavorably to Socrates, mocked the Sermon on the Mount, and openly proclaimed Greek folk religion to be a more joyful and positive human experience than Christian worship of any kind.[10]

Hegel's goal was "to restore the human being again in his totality," and he did not believe Christianity could accomplish this.[11] In 1795, two years after the enthronement of the Goddess of Reason in Notre Dame, Hegel wrote an essay that was an interpretive life of Jesus but not intended for publication. It begins, "Pure reason, incapable of any limitation, is the deity itself."[12]

In this sense, Hegel completely rejected the Christian faith—and its message of hope—as the basis for any effort to "restore" the human being with any success. In its place he believed that philosophy could restore mankind, and his life's work, in a sense, was devoted to devising a philosophical system that would explain all of human history and behavior. The cosmology Hegel devised was immensely complex and intricate, and it has often defied the comprehension of its most devoted students.

In essence, Hegel believed that history was a process by which something called the Absolute Spirit was fulfilling its destiny in the world. Various stages of human development, in the Hegelian view, corresponded to ever-new moments of self-discovery of that Spirit. Progress toward the end of history, Hegel held, took place as the Spirit came to grips with this destiny by expressing itself in art, religion, and philosophy, as well as through the conflicts and wars common to all of history.

The famous Hegelian dialectic, which Karl Marx adapted, grew out of Hegel's sense that historical progress derived from a new synthesis that occurred whenever two opposites collided. Just as two people argue differing points of view and then arrive at a consensus that embraces portions of the arguments of each, so history, or the Spirit of history, in the Hegelian view, marches forward in search of its ultimate fulfillment. Eventually, there would be an end to history: Hegel believed that human society would cease from its contradictions and conflicts.[13]

Meanwhile, Hegel said, philosophy itself must establish a new religion, one that would both embrace the "infinite grief" of human history and yet somehow rise above it.[14] Hope, in effect, was just around the corner.

But what kind of religion? Hegel himself defined it in a number of different ways, most of them philosophically dense even for students experienced with the jargon of philosophical debate. "God is only God insofar as he knows himself," wrote Hegel. "His knowing himself is, furthermore, a self-consciousness in man and man's knowledge of God that goes on to man's knowing himself *in* God."[15]

Hegel was essentially saying, with astonishing hubris, that God was now dependent on man for any role that he might seek to play in the world. Even though Hegel did not explicitly attack Christian beliefs in his public writings, the philosophical system he was constructing out of his philosophical speculation was not only monistic—all is one—but pantheistic as well. In fact, one conservative German theologian, who followed the development of Hegelian thought in Berlin in the 1830s, the decade at whose beginning Hegel died, explicitly labeled Hegelianism pantheism.[16]

Friedrich Engels himself, Karl Marx's decades-long partner in the construction of Marxist theory, acknowledged with mocking approval the interpretation of Hegel as anti-Christian in his satirical poem *The Insolently Threatened yet Miraculously Rescued Bible*. His cynical lines deserve to be quoted at length:

The furious Hegel who'd been speechless all along,
Forthwith rose like a giant and finally gave tongue:
"To Science I've devoted every hour,
I've taught Atheism with all my power,
Self-consciousness upon the Throne I seated,
And thought that God had thereby been defeated."[17]

The 1830s amounted to one of the great intellectual turning points in European history, in world history, and therefore, in the history of hope. Before that pivotal decade, ideas like "philosophy," "history," even

"God," had content that would have been recognizable to thinkers hundreds of years earlier. Even the then newly minted word "communism" fell within a framework of definitions inherited from earlier eras. But after the 1840s, a huge shift in intellectual attitudes took place in Europe, and most importantly in Germany. The consequences of those attitudes were to devastate all of the human race a century later.

WHAT IS GOD? IS GOD MAN?

Karl Marx's collaborator Friedrich Engels, with his usual sharp sense of great moments of change, did not exaggerate when he wrote in 1844: "The question has always previously been: what is God? And German philosophy has answered the question in this sense: God is man."[18]

With the enormous prestige of Hegel's reputation as a philosopher shielding them, a clustering of radical "Young Hegelians" in Berlin decided to take the philosophical logic of Hegelianism as far as it would go. They chose, simply put, to do away with God and with the hope that Jewish and later Christian belief in him had brought into European civilization.

If, after all, God "needed" man for self-realization in the historical sense, as Hegel had proposed, then the entire Christian faith must be founded on philosophical quicksand. How had Christianity arisen at all? Was it not out of a "need" for the human race as a whole to express the belief that the essence of "God" was to be found within mankind? The 1830s and 1840s saw a philosophical assault on Christianity, and implicitly on the Christian view of hope, that was every bit as frenzied as had been the assaults of the eighteenth-century Bible critics on the historical and textual integrity of Holy Scripture.

By far the most influential writer from this group was Ludwig Feuerbach, whose *The Essence of Christianity*, published in 1841, greatly influenced Karl Marx (even though Marx was later to criticize Feuerbach for trying to replace Christianity with a religious concoction of his own) and an entire generation of German atheists. Feuerbach was much less vague in his formulations than Hegel. "Religion itself," he wrote, "... in its essence believes in nothing else than the truth and divinity of human nature."[19]

Hegel had written that history was the self-expression of God in the form of Absolute Spirit. But Feuerbach, a zealous materialist, turned this formulation completely around: God was merely a self-expression of *man* in man's path toward self-consciousness. What was needed for mankind, Feuerbach said, was a philosophy that could entrench man's consciousness of himself as the only real God. He wrote: "The turning point in history will be the moment when man becomes aware that the only God is man himself."[20]

God is dead, and we have killed him.

It is a striking coincidence—if coincidence it is—that Germany, the starting point of the Protestant Reformation and the soaring upsurge in Christian optimism that fueled so many good things in Western history, should have also been the seedbed of so much of mankind's darkness in the last century.

The German Jewish poet Heinrich Heine, whom we have already quoted in discussing Immanuel Kant, looked to the future of the emerging new religion of man in 1834, just three years after the death of Hegel. With startling prescience, he foresaw the devastating evil that would be the end result of the enthronement in Germany of belief in the deity of man. Looking gloomily into the future, Heine predicted:

The natural philosopher will be terrible, for he has allied himself to the primal forces of nature. He can conjure up the demonic powers of ancient German pantheism... and if ever that restraining talisman, the Cross, is shattered, there shall arise once more... that mindless madman's rage of which the Nordic poets sang so much.... I warn you, Frenchman, keep then quite still, and for God's sake do not applaud!![21]

Heine's forebodings obviously applied to the rise of Nazism, a belief system that did indeed have profound roots in occult practices and beliefs, but whose underlying philosophical premise was that man was capable of anything if he but applied his will to it. That viewpoint owed a lot to the writings of Friedrich Nietzsche (1844-1900), whose work contains the most sustained attack on the Christian view of life of any of the prolifically anti-Christian German writers of the nineteenth century. It was Nietzsche who wrote: "God is dead, and we have killed him."[22]

Yet the "death of God" philosophy (and later theology) in the general sense invoked far more than the scourge of Hitler and Nazism, terrible as they were. After Hegel, the dominant impetus of the Western intellectual tradition was the search for hope. However, it was a search that led in directions completely opposite to Christianity.

SIX

Hegel, Marx, Humanism, and Freud

F our major sources of hope arose from the ferment of thought left by Hegel. By far the most important was the transmutation of the Christian and Jewish Messianic idea, through the alchemy of atheism, philosophical determinism, and economic doctrines, into the world of politics. This source, of course, led to Marxism, and in Russia under Lenin, Marxism-Leninism. This belief system looked, for a few decades, as though it would capture the entire world through revolutionary upheavals.

Second was the emergence of widespread optimism about the power of science to solve human problems. This, combined with Darwinian evolutionary theory, provided a basis for a new optimism about human development.

Third was the emergence of the belief that psychology, in particular the ideas of Sigmund Freud, provided the most profound insights yet into the workings of the human psyche. This created possibilities for its cure or "improvement."

Fourth was the introduction of Hindu and Buddhist ideas and exposure to spiritism, through Theosophy, into small but influential circles in British and American society. Theosophy was the entry point for the emergence of the New Age movement in modern times.

All four of these sources of hope have proved to be false. But only the first, Marxism-Leninism, has finally run its course and exists in isolated pockets around the world.

MARXISM AND THE HOPE OF REVOLUTION

"The philosophers," Marx wrote in one of his most quoted of all aphorisms, "have only *interpreted* the world in various ways; the point, however, is to *change* it" (emphasis in original).[1] Marx, in his doctoral dissertation at the University of Berlin (he was only twenty-three when he wrote it), showed that he was grasping for "a great, a world philosophy" that would utterly transform not just human thought but all of world society.[2]

This understanding of philosophy was certainly not friendly to the world into which it was born. As Marx also wrote: "Like Prometheus who stole fire from heaven and began to build houses and settle on the earth, so philosophy, which has evolved so as to impinge on the world, turns itself against the world which it finds."[3]

And how violently it did so. In the most famous of all the works in what became the quasi-religious canon of Marxism-Leninism, *The Communist Manifesto*, Marx and Engels, the joint authors, openly proclaimed the intention of Communists to overthrow the existing social and political order by force.

Since, in the Marxist view, all of human history had been nothing but a struggle for the ownership of production and wealth among different classes, so the resolution of all of mankind's struggles and pain would be accomplished when the final class of all, the propertyless urban proletariat, rose up to overthrow the existing order. Once in power, the proletariat would establish a socialist dictatorship that would ensure the transition to a society in which no further exploitation of one group by another would theoretically be possible. "The proletarians have nothing to lose but their chains," proclaimed the *Manifesto* in another of its universally recognized quotations. "They have a world to win."[4]

The Marxist hope, some have suggested, is in economics. But this is only part of the story. Behind the dream of a world of peace and social justice (once revolutionaries have seized power) is really a spiritual longing—though never acknowledged to be such—for a sense that history itself is working its way toward a final resolution in the Hegelian sense.

One of the most interesting books to be published in the days of the Cold War confrontation between the U.S. and the Soviet Union was *The God That Failed*, an account by several Western former Communists of their initial conversion to Communism and their subsequent disillusionment. A number of the authors describe their falling away from Communism as a loss of faith, the dashing of a hope that had for a time given their lives a sense of purpose and adventure.

In *The God That Failed,* novelist Arthur Koestler wrote of his initial zeal for the Communist cause quite unselfconsciously as a "mental rapture" for "a new star of Bethlehem," and conversely of his disillusionment in these no less biblical terms:

> I served the Communist Party for seven years—the same length of time as Jacob tended Laban's sheep to win Rachel his daughter. When the time was up, the bride was led into his dark tent; only the next morning did he discover that his ardors had been spent not on the lovely Rachel but on the ugly Leah.[5]

The appeal of Communism, like that of all universal religious or pseudo-religious beliefs, transcended racial, linguistic, and cultural barriers. For several decades, it seduced a large number of Western intellectuals—writers, academics, philosophers—men and women who were already so alienated from their own cultural tradition that they readily embraced any alternative to it.

OPIUM OF THE INTELLECTUALS

In an ironic counterplay to Marx's own dictum that religion was "the opium of the people," the late French political analyst Raymond Aron wrote a critical account of Marxism itself in the early 1950s entitled *Opium of the Intellectuals.* American journalist Lincoln Steffens (1866-1936) coined the infamous (because so totally mistaken) phrase describing his visit to the Soviet Union in the 1920s—"I have been over into the future, and it works." From Steffens to the "Sandalistas," sandal-clad, guilt-ridden middle-class Americans who made political pilgrimages to Nicaragua in the 1980s to support the Sandinista revolutionary regime, Americans in particular have been prone to naïveté about the global Marxist experiment in utopia-building.

Yet British, French, Swedes, and other Westerners scarcely lagged behind in revolutionary piety, as long as the social engineering they applauded didn't affect them. Paul Hollander's *Political Pilgrims*[6] is a revealing story of the perennial tendency of idealistic people to admire social progress when it is brought about through tyranny, provided they don't have to live under the authoritarian regime that provides it.

A characteristic of the false hope induced by Communism was always the refusal among its followers around the world to believe nightmarish revelations about Marxist-Leninist rule. When some new atrocity was uncovered—the massacre of Polish officers in Katyn forest in Poland by Stalin's troops in 1940, for example, or the killing fields of Cambodia in the 1970s—there were always excuses offered. If the atrocities were grudgingly acknowledged in some measure to have been true, then they were said to be an aberration of revolutionary practice rather than the logical result of applying revolutionary theory.

When the "Great Terror" of the Stalinist political executions in the Soviet Union of the 1930s had become too well known to discount, many who clung to the Marxist hope realigned their faith, believing there might be an improved version of Communism around the corner in Mao's China.

HOPE IN MAO'S CHINA

Indeed, China's struggle to shake off both Japanese occupation and the legacy of social, economic, and political backwardness through Communism inspired several Westerners, including Americans, to visit the country almost as pilgrims. In a number of cases, those Westerners were so enraptured of the supposed social utopia after 1949 that they abandoned the West altogether and lived in China as adoptive citizens.

One such person, a remarkable American called Sidney Rittenberg, has described both his initial intoxication with the idealism of the Chinese Communist revolution in its very early years, and his subsequent experiences as a victim of its inevitable excesses. Here he is in 1946 in Yanan, northern China, on the point of meeting the almost legendary Chinese Communist leader, Mao Zedong:

> I felt a strange exultation.
>
> Everything around me seemed clean and pure. The people. Their clothes. The building. The music. Even the fierce winds and bleak landscape of Yanan seemed unsullied to me. I was in a place far from the naked greed and corruption I had already seen too much of.[7]

The Marxist-Leninist hope, when stripped of rhetoric and posturing, is very simple: Changed economic structures will bring about not just social justice in the short term but a radically improved society in the long term. Eventually, the theory holds, the dictatorship of the proletariat (the Communist Party dictatorship) will lead to a transition to Communism, an ideal social, political, and economic state of affairs that neither Marx nor any other Communist ever quite defined.

Perhaps the closest Marx himself came to depicting it was to describe it as a transition from "the realm of necessity" (where economic relationships in society were determined by the exploitation of man by man allegedly inherent in capitalism) to the "realm of freedom." The banner of such a society, he wrote elsewhere, was to be "from each according to his ability, to each according to his needs."[8]

But as everyone now knows, the Communist hope in the Soviet Union was a bitter, tragic mishmash of political terror and murder, mass starvation, labor camps, economic incompetence, deprivation, cultural stagnation, and finally perhaps the worst degree of cynicism that any society in history has ever experienced at the popular level. When the hammer and sickle flag was pulled down from atop the Kremlin for the last time in December 1991, very few even in the Communist Party were genuinely sorry. Faith had long since departed from Moscow's version of Marxism-Leninism, and hope had vanished even earlier.

But what about other Communist countries? Eastern Europe, of course, threw off its Communist yoke even earlier, in 1989, in a paroxysm of joy reminiscent of someone finally throwing off a seemingly endless bout of flu. Only in Cuba, where Marxist-Leninism has acquired a seemingly genetic sheen of anti-*yanqui* resentment, has Communism survived in power outside of East Asia. There, of course, the Communist hope was from the beginning linked to hatred of colonialism.

The xenophobic tyranny of Kim Il-sung and his son Kim Jong-il in North Korea, for example, was relentlessly rationalized throughout its nearly five decades in power by its claim to have single-handedly vanquished Japanese colonialism. Meanwhile, in Vietnam, Laos, and Cambodia, first the legacy of the anti-French struggle for independence and then the militarization of society in the face of the U.S. military involvement in the region helped maintain a toehold in power for Communist regimes that became unpopular almost as soon as they overthrew their non-Communist rivals.

The Communist hope for China at first appeared to be broadly accepted by many Chinese. When Mao Zedong proclaimed the Chinese People's Republic atop the Tiananmen rostrum in October 1949, the majority of his compatriots, exhausted by Japanese occupation and then a brutal civil war, seemed willing to accept almost any regime that could restore order, establish a minimum of social justice, and maintain China's global independence. By the early 1960s, however, three things were apparent, even to the most fanatical Chinese believers in the Marxist-Leninist canon:

First, the Soviet experiment had gone badly off course.

Second, Mao Zedong himself had made dangerous mistakes in governing his country.

Third, a new class of bureaucrats had emerged in power, much less interested in the future advent of Communism than the present enjoyment of bureaucratic privileges.

HOPE IN THE LITTLE RED BOOK

Mao responded to political opposition as well as the problem of bureaucratic greed by launching the Cultural Revolution (1966-1969, but with lingering effects through 1976). This was perhaps the most radical attempt in history to force an entire country through a religious revolution, albeit one that was supposedly atheistic. For months at a time, millions of young Chinese seemed to be in the thrall of a Messianic zeal that looked at first like the discovery of a genuine new hope for themselves and for China.

Certainly they had embraced a new faith, a zealous idolatry of Mao Zedong, China's leader, that projected onto him literally supernatural powers. As the entire country of more than 700 million ground to a halt, teenagers by the hundreds of thousands stormed around the country waving, reading from, and memorizing the *Little Red Book,* or to give it its precise name, *Quotations from Chairman Mao.*

Had China indeed uncovered some secret of human behavior or thought that might change not only itself, but the world as a whole? "Once Mao Zedong's thought is grasped by the broad masses," declared Mao's then Defense Minister, Lin Biao, in his foreword to the second edition of the book, "it becomes an inexhaustible source of strength and a spiritual atom bomb of infinite power."[9]

"Every sentence of Chairman Mao's is truth," Lin added elsewhere, "and carries more weight than 10,000 other sentences."[10] That supposed "truth" inspired Chinese of all ages and professions to superhuman feats of self-sacrifice or accomplishment.

But the hope engendered by Mao's Cultural Revolution proved as elusive and short-lived as every other guise of the Marxist-Leninist promise had been, even though some Westerners were momentarily deceived. "Maoism," said one entranced observer at the time, "is a serious call to socially responsible moral conduct which has a great deal in common with Christian rectitude, especially in its Protestant and Victorian embodiment."[11]

If the "oppressed" have demonstrated anything in the past decade, it is that every time they have an opportunity to pass up the Communist hope, they do so.

"Christian rectitude"? Hardly. One Christian who suffered torture under the supposedly "socially responsible" Red Guards, who murdered her daughter, was Nien Cheng, author of *Life and Death in Shanghai*. Nien, like millions of others, was sadistically beaten, tortured, falsely accused of lunatic criminal acts for years on end, and released only after the creator of all the insanity, Mao Zedong, had himself died and his closest followers had been arrested. "To people who have not dealt with such men as the Maoists," she writes, "my persistent effort to fight back against my persecutors may seem futile and pointless. But the Maoists were essentially bullies. If I had allowed them to insult me at will, they would have been encouraged to go further."[12]

Yet despite this, Maoism, with its total rejection of any form of property ownership and its fearsome egalitarianism, somehow lingered on even outside China as Communism's last, best hope. "Revolution is the hope of the hopeless," proclaims the Revolutionary Communist Party in posters it still bravely puts up in little bookstore outposts across the U.S. "Proletarian revolution," its *New Programme and New Constitution* announced in 1981, is "the long-cherished hope of the oppressed."[13]

If the "oppressed" have demonstrated anything in the past decade, it is that every time they have an opportunity to pass up the Communist hope, they do so. In 1989 some stood in front of tanks in the same Tiananmen Square where Mao had first announced the Chinese revolution. To this day others entrust their lives to leaky rafts on Cuban beaches in their desperate effort to reach the U.S.

SCIENCE AND THE RISE OF ATHEISTIC HUMANISM

One of the oddest things about Marx, in retrospect, is that he called his doctrine "scientific socialism." This was to distinguish it from other brands of socialism, particularly in France, that Marx sneeringly labeled as "utopian" because they did not arrive festooned with the heavy baggage of German philosophy, economic research, and footnotes by the hundreds.

In the nineteenth century, the word *scientific* had an almost entirely positive ring to it in both Europe and the U.S. Progress in several different scientific fields was phenomenal. In physics, Newton's corpuscular theory of light was replaced by the wave theory put forward by Thomas Young and Augustine Fresnel. The Englishman Michael Faraday (a committed Christian, incidentally) experimented with electro-magnetism. The German Wilhelm Roentgen discovered X-rays, and huge progress was made in the study of atomic weights and the molecular structure of cells.

Overshadowing all of these discoveries, however, was the impact of Charles Darwin. After *On the Origin of Species* appeared in 1859, science was not only no longer on the defensive against theology, as it had been from the days of Copernicus (1473-1543). It now openly stood against philosophical positions supportive of a belief in God.

The most obvious and best-known result of the Darwinian evolution-ary theory was the powerful scientific challenge to the hitherto accepted scheme of biblical chronology. An earth that was only six thousand to seven thousand years old (if biblical time schemes were accepted literally) did not jibe with the findings in several areas of science, but especially in botany, biology, and geology, which suggested a far longer time frame of natural and human evolution.

Meanwhile, the notion of *natural selection,* Darwin's term to explain why some natural species such as dinosaurs had become extinct, found almost instant echoes in the fields of sociology and politics. Karl Marx, for example, whose own evolutionary concept of history derived from Hegel's philosophy, was so struck by what he presumed to be Darwin's confirmation in natural history of his own theory of surplus value that he asked if he could dedicate the first volume of *Das Kapital* to the Englishman. Darwin politely declined. The sociologist Herbert Spencer, however, coined the term "survival of the fittest" to describe not just the world of biology, but all human societies, in terms of an endless Darwinian struggle of various groups to prevail against each other.

At one level, the crushing blow seemingly aimed at the Christian hope by the scientific discoveries of the nineteenth century appeared to offer a new, man-made hope. If evolution in the natural arena meant increasingly more adaptive and sophisticated species, was there not a corollary in the evolution of human society? The tradition of secular humanism, indeed, has answered this question in the affirmative ever since the Darwinian watershed in Western thought.

Darwin himself was moderately optimistic that the process of evolution he thought to be still operative within mankind was moving in a positive direction. In his important work tellingly entitled *The Descent of Man* (1871), he wrote:

Man may be excused for feeling some pride at having risen, though not through his own exertions, to the very summit of the organic scale: and the fact of his having thus risen, instead of having been aboriginally placed there, may give him hope for a still higher destiny in the distant future.

But he was not convinced that all would work out for the best. "With his god-like intellect which has penetrated into the movements and constitution of the solar system—with all these exalted powers," Darwin concluded almost somberly in his book, "man still bears in his bodily frame the indelible stamp of his lowly origin."[14]

"WE MUST SAVE OURSELVES"

A century later, the Darwinian hypothesis of human origins had become so universally enthroned in schools and universities in the Western world (and in the world of Karl Marx's Communist legacy too), that all trace of Darwin's reservations had vanished in the presentation of it. With a book and a widely viewed TV series, anthropologist and philosopher Jacob Bronowsky turned Darwin's own title on its head with his own *The Ascent of Man* (1973). No longer cautious and modest in depicting the human condition within nature, Bronowsky exulted:

We are nature's unique experiment to make the rational intelligence prove itself sounder than the reflex. Knowledge is our destiny. Self-knowledge, at last bringing together the experience of the arts and the explanation of science, waits ahead of us.[15]

What is curious about this triumphalism is that secular humanism somehow managed to preserve its public optimism about the human condition in the face of overwhelming twentieth-century evidence that even Darwin's doubts for the human future were understated. On the surface, secular humanism today meekly describes itself as "a perspective on man and nature that is derived from the natural, biological, and behavioral sciences."[16]

W *e can discover no divine purpose or providence for the human species....* *No deity will save us; we must save ourselves.*

That is a very modest definition. *Humanist Manifesto II,* signed in 1973 by 275 "intellectuals of thought and action," affirms categorically, "We can discover no divine purpose or providence for the human species. While there is much that we do not know, humans are responsible for what we are or will become. No deity will save us; we must save ourselves."[17]

The original *Humanist Manifesto* was signed in 1933, a poignant year, in retrospect, to be so upbeat about the human potential for good. It was in 1933 that Adolf Hitler came to power and began the process that led to the slaughter of scores of millions of people in his own country and throughout Europe. There wasn't a lot of "saving" being done for the victims of Hitler's demonic ambitions.

Nonetheless, forty years later, the second of the two humanist manifestos speaks as though nothing in human experience has modified the belief that, by making decisions without any regard to higher authority than man, somehow there is assurance of human progress, and hope for the race as a whole. *Humanist Manifesto II* derides "traditional moral codes" as "false 'theologies of hope,'" of no more value than the "messianic ideologies" that have dominated the twentieth century (presumably Nazism and Communism).[18] How striking that the very messianic ideologies that brought about the Holocaust in Germany and Nazi-occupied Europe and the Great Terror of Stalinism in the Soviet Union derived their roots from exactly the same Rationalist assault upon Christianity that is the philosophical basis of today's secular humanism.

Today's humanists boldly demand that ethics should be "autonomous and situational, needing no theological or ideological sanction."[19] But if there are no philosophical reasons for setting specific constraints on human behavior among "good people"—middle-class Americans, including humanists, who lament the breakdown of family life as much as humanist writer Paul Kurtz says he does[20]—then on what moral basis can one condemn, much less rein in, the behavior of beasts like Hitler and Stalin?

"What, at bottom, is the whole of modern philosophy doing?" asked the philosopher Friedrich Nietzsche in 1886, sneering at Christianity for resembling "a protracted suicide of reason."[21] Nietzsche's own response: "Modern philosophy, as an epistemological skepticism, is, covertly or openly, *anti-Christian:* although, to speak to more refined ears, by no means anti-religious [italics in original]."[22]

A HUMANIST "VISION OF HOPE"

What hope do the humanists offer instead? "We strive for the good life, here and now," is one blunt response in *Humanist Manifesto II.* To this is added an impressive agenda of programs that would seem, if implemented, to take care of almost everything that has troubled human history since the beginning of time:

> To control our environment, conquer poverty, markedly reduce disease, extend our life span, significantly modify our behavior, alter the course of human evolution and cultural development, unlock vast new powers and provide humankind with unparalleled opportunity for achieving an abundant and meaningful life.[23]

The basis for such grandiose ambitions, according to *Humanist Manifesto I,* is "a design for a secular society on a planetary scale." That design, the manifesto goes on, "is a vision for hope, a direction for satisfying survival."[24]

There is no need to question the sincerity of humanists like Kurtz, who may sincerely and in his own way try to lead the "good" life. But there is every reason to question the rationality of their beliefs. To believe that the human race will collectively acquire the moderation, self-restraint, and wisdom required for the humanist program primarily by abandoning hope in other directions requires far more faith in human benevolence than any average believer in God has to deploy in a lifetime.

Humanists are usually quick to note how much harm has been done in the world by fanatically motivated religious believers at different times. Certainly damage has been done by religious zealotry, including that of Christians. But humanists are much slower to acknowledge that the mass slaughter unleashed in the world by atheistic regimes in the twentieth century alone exceeds by a factor of several times all of the victims of religious intolerance throughout the whole of preceding human history.

The utter falseness of the optimism of the humanist position has been articulated many times this century, most eloquently by those who have been humanists themselves. The famous science fiction writer H.G. Wells (*The Time Machine* [1895], *The War of the Worlds* [1898]) had a truly prophetic understanding of the power of science to change people's lives, yet a wildly unrealistic trust in humanity's ability to deploy such power wisely. Amazingly, *The Outline of History* that Wells published in 1920, despite the horrors of World War I, was full of evolution-based idealism about the glorious future in front of humanity. But in 1945, a year before his death, and with the knowledge of both the destructive power of the atomic bomb and Hitler's unquenchably evil genius still fresh, Wells entitled his final book *The Mind at the End of Its Tether*. In it he wrote, "There is no way out, or around, or through the impasse. It is the end."[25]

In many ways the greatest refutation of the humanist hope is found in the honest articulation of what humanists ultimately believe about human destiny. In the end, they believe, humanity will simply die out, the chance victim of the inexorable law of death and decay as much as the chance beneficiary of the chance incident of its birth. Here is the English philosopher Bertrand Russell, in *Why I Am Not a Christian:*

> That man is the product of causes which had no prevision of the end they were achieving; that his origin, his growth, his hopes and fears, his loves and beliefs, are but the outcome of accidental collocations of atoms; that no fire, no heroism, no intensity of thought and feeling, can preserve an individual life beyond the grave... that all the noonday brightness of human genius, are destined to extinction in the vast death of the solar system, and that the whole temple of man's achievement must inevitably be buried underneath the debris of a universe in ruins—all these things, if not quite beyond dispute, are yet so nearly certain that no philosophy that rejects them can hope to stand.[26]

Russell, of course, has it exactly the wrong way round. The humanist view on the one hand holds to the ultimate metaphysical hopelessness of life so eloquently expressed by Russell. Yet, on the other, it clings to an entirely irrational hope that human beings will somehow get it all right in the end. Some hope.

Secular humanism, considered in its historical context, is in the direct line of descent of Rationalist and atheistic thinkers going back to the Enlightenment and earlier. It drew some strength from the anti-Christian writings of Hegel's followers, but in its relatively mild-mannered public garb today, it is more the heir of Darwin and Huxley, Wells and Russell than of Feuerbach or Marx. At various times it has wrapped itself in the garb of a secular faith. Today, it offers a hope hinged to optimism about human nature in the face of relentlessly accumulating evidence that human nature is truly fallible and truly "fallen."

PSYCHOLOGY AND HOPE IN THE SELF

The third of the four major sources of hope to flow out of the nineteenth century was modern psychology. From Freud and William James onward, psychology has sometimes presented itself as amounting to not just a new hope for solving human problems but a panacea for everything that has ever afflicted the human race.

There is a broad consensus among historians that Marx and Freud have dominated the entire intellectual universe of our century. One offered salvation for humanity through changed structures of society; the other proposed to cure its woes by understanding, and then altering, the inner nature of the human psyche. Both, though Jewish, were atheists and materialists who had been profoundly influenced by Ludwig Feuerbach. Both based their new world views squarely on a rejection of any form of the supernatural or worship of God. In the end, Marx and Freud sought not just to banish traditional Jewish and Christian faith in God but to replace it with completely new secular systems of belief.

We have already looked at the Marxist-Leninist pseudo-religion, particularly in its Maoist form, with revolution as the "hope of the hopeless," complete with a sort of parody of Christian theology. Marxists used to write and speak of an all-powerful History in terms reminiscent of the Christian belief in God the Father, of the proletariat as the Suffering

Savior, the Communist Party as the priesthood, and the writings of Marx, Engels, and Lenin (and sometimes Stalin and Mao) as Holy Scripture.

Of course, there were differences between these pseudo-religions. Psychology—Freudianism in particular—could never triumph in the West as a public idolatry in the way that government oppression enabled Marxism to become in countries where Communists attained power. Yet in its own way, psychology has succeeded in becoming the ultimate substitute religion of modern times. This is especially so in the U.S., which contains one-third of all the psychologists on earth. "Psychology," says Paul Vitz, a psychologist who has analyzed his own profession, "has become a religion... a secular cult of the self... more specifically, a form of secular humanism based on the rejection of God and the worship of the self."[27]

HOPE IN FREUD AND JUNG

It can hardly be disputed that none of this would have happened without Sigmund Freud (1856-1939). From such terms as "Oedipus complex," "the unconscious mind," "the id and the superego," and even "Freudian slip," the impact of Freud's view of the human psyche is impossible to escape today, even among the vast majority of people who have never read a word of Freud.

Freud's greatest impact was in two arenas: that of exploration of the deepest motivations of the human mind and emotions, and psychotherapy, where the "talking cure," as it was first called, demonstrated that

> *Freud saw himself as a "new Moses" who would lead the human race out of its age-long fascination with religious belief into a new age of self-enlightenment.*

patients could indeed be relieved—and sometimes apparently cured—of deep emotional stress and trauma through the application of analysis during therapy sessions.

Freud single-handedly contributed to a radical alteration of prevailing views of human nature. At the same time, his writings and psychotherapeutic methods were adopted by disciples, and eventually rivals, in a way that transformed not just the young science of psychology, but philosophy itself.

To begin with, Freud was a convinced materialist, influenced profoundly by both Ludwig Feuerbach and Charles Darwin. At the same
time, he saw himself as a "new Moses" who would lead the human race
out of its age-long fascination with religious belief into a new age of self-
enlightenment. Though many of Freud's contemporaries disagreed with
his open rejection of religious faith, particularly in his book *The Future of
an Illusion* (1927), they found compelling his description of the irrational
in human nature.

He described the psyche as being locked in a battle between the
instinct of aggression, which leads to death, and the sex instinct (Eros),
which Freud viewed as life-producing. Freud viewed man's search for
perfection as a repressed sexual instinct demanding satisfaction.[28] At the
same time, he thought civilization was constantly menaced with
disintegration because of the universal human instinct of aggression;
culture itself was "the struggle between Eros and death, between the
instincts of life and the instincts of destruction."[29]

In an important way Freud dispelled the facile optimism about human
progress that had dominated the materialist philosophers of the eighteenth and nineteenth centuries. He was a Darwinian who believed that
evolution was basically an accident of nature. However, illogically, Freud
concluded that "eternal Eros" would somehow exert itself to counter-
balance the negative human impact of the death instinct of aggression.[30]

Freud's powerful personality may have protected him from the gloomy
implications of his theories of human personality. His most important
followers, however, soon diverged from him in the search for a message of
hope deep within the human psyche. By far the most important of these,
and later a bitter rival, was Carl Jung (1875-1961), who had accompanied
Freud on the Austrian's first visit to the U.S. in 1909.

Jung's theories are too complex to explain satisfactorily in a short space
(though it's worth noting that he developed the concepts of extroverted
and introverted personalities, and the word "complex" as a noun was
coined by him), but two of his contributions had immense influence on
the change in direction that post-Freudian psychology took.

First, he argued that there was a "collective unconscious" of the entire
human race, a sort of pan-human unconscious memory that accounted
for many of the recurrent themes of religious mythology in various
cultures around the world.

Second, he stressed the importance of discovery of the true self as the
key to mental health, the key, in effect, to human hope.

In both of these areas, Jung not only departed from the strictly materialist interpretation of human behavior offered by Freud. He also opened the door to self-worship in a way that led almost immediately back to the ancient Christian heresy of Gnosticism, and thence to pantheism. That directly leads us to the subject of New Age and the tragically false hope it offers.

SEVEN

Gnosticism, Self-Worship, and the New Age

G nosticism was a system of thought that grew up in the early years of Christianity from a variety of sources. These included the Greek mystery cults, the Persian religion of Zoroastrianism, the Jewish occult writings known as the Kabbalah, and perhaps even the pantheism of Hinduism. Gnosticism flatly repudiated two aspects of the Christian view: God's incarnation as a man in the person of Jesus Christ, and the fundamental flaw in human beings that Christians call sin. Because Gnosticism appealed to the innate human fascination with the mysterious, and because it subtly suggested that a special, elitist kind of knowledge (the Greek word *gnosis*) rather than faith was the key to salvation, it was a profoundly serious threat to Christian orthodoxy in the second and third centuries.

JUNG AND HIS MYSTERY CULT

Gnostics believed that matter itself was evil but that imprisoned within every human being there was a divine seed or spark that needed to be set free. Salvation, in the Gnostic sense, could be accomplished through the liberating gnosis, which was itself sometimes to be reached by practicing extreme forms of asceticism (long fasts, for example). The parallels with ancient Indian thought are so striking that the best-known popularizer of Gnosticism in recent years, the scholar Elaine Pagels, cannot resist asking the obvious question:

Does not such teaching—the identity of the divine and human, the concern with illusion and enlightenment, the founder who is presented not as Lord, but as spiritual guide—sound more Eastern than Western?

Some scholars have suggested that if the names were changed, the "living Buddha" appropriately could say what the Gospel of Thomas [a major Gnostic work] attributes to the living Jesus. Could Hindu or Buddhist tradition have influenced gnosticism?[1]

Carl Jung was fascinated with Gnosticism, as Pagels herself notes with some enthusiasm,[2] but what is far more astonishing is that he did not confine his interest to mere intellectual curiosity. Jung actually founded his own secret cult in which a small group of disciples was told that the path to personality transformation was through self-deification.

He encouraged his patients to embark on visionary journeys to "the Land of the Dead" to consult with their ancestors. He himself claimed that he had experienced becoming a god. He said that in 1913 he had become a combination of Christ and a lion-headed deity from an ancient Hellenistic mystery cult. Jung told a small, confidential group of disciples that he wanted to see the development of a spiritual elite similar to a pagan spiritual "brotherhood" mentioned in a poem by Goethe, using as its symbol a cross wound with roses.[3]

> Gnostics believed that matter itself was evil but that imprisoned within every human being there was a divine seed or spark that needed to be set free.

In short, one of the most highly influential figures in the search of psychology to solve the deepest problems of the human soul and discover a new hope for twentieth-century mankind was in no way a Rationalist of the eighteenth, or nineteenth-century variety, mocking religion as unscientific. Rather, he was a man who had opened himself to the powers of paganism and perhaps even, through quasi-spiritist experiences, to direct experiences of the occult.

What ardent materialists and secularists of every generation have always failed to grasp is that, in slamming shut the door on Jewish and Christian supernaturalism, they have caused other windows of supernatural human experience to rattle open, windows through which the occult and the openly demonic have intruded into the human heart.

This did not happen right away. Jung and other post-Freudian psychologists who focused on the self spent several decades introducing the concept of the self as the key to happiness to broad, popular audiences. Only after the investigation, the celebration, and eventually the worship of the self had taken root in popular self-help literature did elements of Gnosticism, pantheism, and even channeling begin to seep in. Before that happened, though, the self-theorists had conducted a sustained war upon orthodox Christian belief and succeeded partially in co-opting much of liberal Protestant theology in their cause. The intention was to create a new, post-Christian hope; the result was to nudge the engine of Western culture closer yet to full-fledged idolatry.

HOPE IN THE GOODNESS OF MAN

One of the most important self-theorists was Erich Fromm (1900-1980). Originally a follower of Freud, Fromm quickly took issue with Freud's harsh view that humanity vacillated between instincts of aggression on the one hand and instincts of life (e.g., sex) on the other. He concluded that human nature was basically good and that self-knowledge could unlock the potentialities for benevolent behavior that were imprisoned beneath layers of self-ignorance or fear in most people. He admitted that if the Christian doctrine of original sin were true, his own theory would have no value at all. He wrote:

> The position taken by humanistic ethics that man is able to know what is good and act accordingly on the strength of his natural potentialities and of his reason would be untenable, if the dogma of man's natural evilness were true.[4]

It is therefore not surprising that Fromm devoted considerable space in his writings to attacking Christian belief head-on. The titles of two of his books are highly suggestive in this connection: *The Dogma of Christ and Other Essays* (1963), and *You Shall Be as Gods* (1966).

The psychologist Paul Vitz has taken a highly critical view of Fromm's self-theory, pointing out how flawed Fromm's understanding of the world of nature really was. Fromm, for example, completely overlooked the phenomenon of male primates arbitrarily killing their own young.[5] Fromm nevertheless to the end of his life clung to the view that human behavior was fundamentally good and needed only to understand itself better.

Fromm's last book was actually called *The Revolution of Hope* (1968).

In effect, he suggested that hope could come from no other source than human nature itself. All we needed to do was to have a better grasp of how it worked for wonderful new kinds of behavior to spring forth. But after decades of self-obsession by a prominent school of Western psychology, there is not the slightest evidence for the validity of this kind of hope.

THE QUEST FOR SELF-REALIZATION

Other theorists of self include Carl Rogers (1902-1980), Abraham Maslow (1908-1970), and Rollo May (1909-1994), all of whom in different ways advanced the beneficent view of human behavior deep into American popular culture. Rogers was influenced by the thought of the American educationist John Dewey (1859-1952), whose work in both psychology and philosophy has caused him to be considered a cofounder of the quintessentially American philosophical school known as Pragmatism. Simplifying their thought greatly, pragmatist philosophers tend to believe that whatever "works" is "true." Rogers devised what he called "non-directive therapy," and this laid the foundation for the enthusiasm for "encounter groups" in the 1970s and 1980s.

Rogers, moreover, claimed to be opposed to all fixed doctrines of religion or psychology, but he himself made into a new dogma the belief that psychology had rendered traditional religion obsolete. Maslow, an atheist, took the theme of self-actualization or self-realization one step further. His Gestalt therapy insisted that questions of moral right and wrong were simply irrelevant to issues of personal psychological health. In effect, human beings could turn themselves into their own deities to make decisions on right and wrong: the determining factor was what decisions best served their self-actualization.

Rollo May carried on the search for hope in the realm of self-discovery. He was one of the first to blend the new self psychology with liberal Protestant theology, which he became familiar with while studying at New York's Union Theological Seminary. Ironically—for May was yet another optimist about human nature—he was also influenced by the philosophy of existentialism, whose leading exponents were the French writers Jean-Paul Sartre (1905-1980) and Albert Camus (1913-1960).

Sartre and Camus wrote, one through philosophical books and plays, the other primarily through novels, about the absurdity and meaninglessness of life. Sartre, in fact, became a champion for a variety of leftist political causes. An atheist like Camus, he was caught in the philosophical trap of how to demonstrate that any one cause had greater value than any other. He concluded that, if man were to have any worthwhile status, he would need to grab hold of the attributes of divinity. Sartre wrote: "To be man means to reach toward being God. Or if you prefer, man fundamentally is the desire to be God."[6]

Camus, a brilliantly talented novelist, raised fundamental questions of meaning and morality in books that have fed the appetite of generations of U.S. college students for a sort of theology of rebellion. For Camus, the only philosophical question of any importance was whether to commit suicide.[7] Ultimately, he died relatively young, at the age of forty-seven, in an accident.

The dead-end street that led out of that suicide question of Camus is perhaps best exemplified by a poster of the Seattle grunge rock group Nirvana, which features a photo of group leader Kurt Cobain and the words of a song recorded by Nirvana but never released. The song was entitled "I hate myself and I want to die."

Cobain told reporters that the recording had been satirical. "I thought it was a funny title," he recalled. But in April 1994, it wasn't funny anymore: Kurt Cobain blew his brains out with a shotgun, leaving a wife and small child. So much for the results of self-deification in a universe devoid of any intrinsic meaning or value.

HOPE IN POSITIVE THINKING

Of course, not all these self-theories had such dire consequences, particularly when allied to an optimistic individualism restrained by traditional morality and a sense of social duty. The quintessentially American phenomenon of positive thinking has had mixed consequences. At its most innocent, it has simply energized people to curb their emotions of anger or pessimism and cultivate common kindness and honesty. But a more sinister stream of the positive mental attitude school of thought, especially popular among some business executives, has been highly narcissistic, selfish, and openly idolatrous.

In its most innocent guise, positive thinking is simply a common-sense celebration of an obvious and age-old human phenomenon: a positive mental attitude to virtually anything in life will yield better results than ruminating on past setbacks or future potential catastrophes. Rugged American individualism and the can-do attitude toward frontier exploration in the nineteenth century also produced a uniquely American literary form of celebrating self in harmony with nature. Ralph Waldo Emerson (1803-1882) may be the best-loved of such thinkers.

But there is a thin, invisible line between a healthy, upbeat approach to life in its often tragic complexity, and a self-centered preoccupation with one's own feelings about the common challenges of ordinary living. Walt Whitman (1802-1847), a poet whom many have considered the very emblem of American cocky individualism, wrote quite unselfconsciously a poem glorifying his own eccentricity. It begins, "I celebrate myself..."[8]

When individualism was celebrated within an understanding that it must not violate the ordinary feelings of others, it was not particularly harmful. America was still big enough and expansive enough to embrace to her bosom a wide variety of often highly creative individualists. But by the early twentieth century, the restraints that an inherited sense of Christian and social duty had imposed on individualism were being challenged. Ironically, the place of confrontation was at least partly at Protestant Christian seminaries themselves.

At the prestigious and influential Union Theological Seminary in New York, for example, the self-theories gained ground in ways that eclipsed the importance of the Christian morality supposedly taught there. One Union student was Harry Emerson Fosdick (1878-1969), who decided that self-realization was a more important goal in life than, say, serving God or working for the building of God's Kingdom. Fosdick's most popular book, *On Being a Real Person* (1943), legitimized for thousands of his readers the view that realization of the self was not only the healthiest approach to life's challenges but was theologically and philosophically legitimate as well.

"The central business of every human being is to be a real person," he wrote. It was not a simple process, he explained, but one that would entail "a perpetual process of becoming."[9] But exactly what is "real," and how would anyone ever know when he or she had experienced a satisfactory degree of "becoming"?

Because there simply is no clear answer to this question, the self-realization concept, if pursued with all one's might, must always be a potentially bottomless pit. It must inevitably lead either to self-idolatry, or to despair, or to both, whether proposed in bluntly atheistic, humanistic terms or garnished with the artificial sweeteners of Christian terminology.

THE POWER OF THE MIND

This raises a difficult question. How does one assess the thought and methodology of Norman Vincent Peale? He is easily the most popular and successful positive thinking exponent in the second half of the twentieth century, and in a sense Fosdick's successor. Peale's books have sold in the millions in dozens of languages. His first runaway best-seller, *The Power of Positive Thinking* (1952), unleashed an entire publishing cottage industry of "positive mental attitude" books in the self-help category. Many were by Peale himself, many by others who profited by repackaging the same "positive" principles.

A handful of positive mental attitude exponents, even though endorsed by Peale, moved out of the ethical and religious boundaries of the Judeo-Christian tradition altogether. Napoleon Hill's (1883-1970) ideas for *Think and Grow Rich* were, according to his own testimony, given to him by "Ascended Masters," in effect, demonic spirit guides with whom he made contact by occultic means (presumably channeling, seances, trances, or other forms of divination).[10]

Hill's view of the value of religious belief is very different from Peale's. For Hill, all faith was merely "a state of mind" that a person may "develop at will." His final source of power is something called "Infinite Intelligence," an impersonal entity that has nothing at all in common with the personal God of Judaism and Christianity.[11] The question is, therefore, how valid are Peale's ideas in arriving at a truly reliable basis for hope?

The answer is not as simple as one would wish. At one point in his career, Peale himself appeared to have embraced fully the doctrines of self-realization. "The greatest day in any individual's life is when he begins for the first time to realize himself," he said in 1937.[12] *The Power of Positive Thinking* begins "Believe in yourself! Have faith in your abilities!"[13]

Yet Peale not only never repudiated his Christian beliefs within the Presbyterian tradition, he often took pains to proclaim within his books the orthodox Christian position on sin and salvation. He was also far from idolizing the self as secular self-theorists did. In fact, Peale makes it clear that it is only through a change of heart after conversion to Jesus Christ that a person can acquire a truly long-term optimistic attitude toward life.[14]

This is the position also held—though at times it is not self-evident—by today's most popular positive thinking advocate within the Christian tradition, Robert Schuller. A flamboyant preacher and speaker with a huge television audience and readers of his books in the millions, Schuller has been criticized by some evangelical Christians for blending into his upbeat sermons and messages elements of Eastern mysticism, including words of praise for the value of chanting Eastern mantras.[15]

But Schuller's view on hope is not New Age at all. In a section entitled "Faith is... replacing worry with hope" in his book with the thoroughly boosterish title *Success Is Never Ending, Failure Is Never Final*, Schuller bases thoughts on hope entirely on biblical Scripture, citing Matthew 6:25-32 ("Therefore I tell you, do not worry about your life, what you will eat or drink; or about your body, what you will wear"), telling his readers:

> Hope is a phenomenon. Faith replaces worry with hope, and no psychiatrist knows what it is. We only know what it does to people. It makes gray skin pink, dull eyes sparkle, and releases healing forces into the body itself!
>
> Affirmation: Today I'm going to walk the walk of faith. My faith will take action as I replace worry with hope.
>
> And what's hope? Holding on, praying expectantly!
>
> Good-by, [sic] worry! Hello, hope![16]

Whatever Schuller's lack of caution about non-Christian practices like mantras, his concept of hope seems to be based squarely on a biblical worldview. This is quite the opposite of the last of the movements in the search for hope that began in psychology but ended up throwing itself headlong into the New Age. What is the final fling of humanistic optimism? Self-esteem and the search for human potential.

HOPE IN SELF-ESTEEM

Many of us may be tempted to dismiss the whole "self-esteem" movement with a bit of a giggle. Since California was the first state to finance a state commission to study the concept back in the late 1980s, with the California Task Force to Promote Self-Esteem and Personal and Social Responsibility, reporters have tended to begin stories describing the movement with phrases like, "Hold on to your hot tubs." California, after all, has often been the breeding ground of some of the oddest cults, belief systems, and practices of American life.

The problem of the self-esteem issue, however, is simple: While an absence of self-esteem clearly does affect people's behavior in a negative way, promoting the "self" regardless of ethical and moral issues or of objective standards of accomplishment is tantamount to believing that it is a car's exhaust, rather than its engine, that causes it to move forward. No dose of self-esteem therapy is going to solve major national social problems like crime, rising illegitimacy, and a declining standard of education.

Paul Vitz, a vigorous critic of the self-esteem movement, dryly notes that there are plenty of inner-city drug dealers who demonstrate no evidence of low self-esteem. He also points to a 1989 study of mathematical skills of high school students in eight countries, in which Korean students ranked highest and American students lowest. When the students were all asked to rate themselves subjectively in their math skills, the Americans nevertheless rated themselves the highest and the Koreans thought they must be the worst. Vitz comments:

> What is wrong with the concept of self-esteem? Lots—and it is fundamental in nature. There have been thousands of psychological studies on self-esteem.... The bottom line is that no agreed-upon definition or agreed-upon measure of self-esteem exists, and whatever it is, no reliable evidence supports self-esteem scores meaning much at all anyways. There is no evidence that self-esteem reliably causes anything—indeed lots of people with little of it have achieved a great deal in one dimension or another.[17]

The self-esteem movement has nevertheless continued to gather a lot of momentum. One reason is the sheer attractiveness of thinking and talking about oneself. Another is the prominence of one its most vigorous advocates, the feminist and former editor of *Ms.* magazine, Gloria Steinem. An active and outspoken speaker, Steinem titled one of her recent books *Revolution from Within: A Book of Self-Esteem.* The points she makes about self-esteem are revealing:

> Far from being a product of California-think or a selfish Me Generation, it goes beyond the West and modern individualism, it is as old and universal as humanity itself.[18]

Steinem correctly observes that both Plato and Aristotle had advocated a rational form of self-love as a crucial condition for general human happiness. But her own concept of self-esteem goes far beyond this. What she overlooks is that healthy notions of the self found a place in Western civilization because they were implicitly balanced by restraining notions of duty and selflessness. Steinem sets the starting-point for her understanding of self-esteem squarely in—where else?—Hinduism and Gnosticism. She writes:

> The idea that self-knowledge was God-knowledge—that the self was a microcosm of the universe, and that knowing the self was our individual way of knowing the mind of God—was central to the origins of Hinduism, and thus to Buddhism, Sufism, and the many other religions that sprang from it.[19]

Steinem cites approvingly from Pagels' book *The Gnostic Gospels* words attributed to Jesus in pseudo-scriptures written some two hundred years after his death and uniformly rejected by the early Church as both wholesale inventions and flat-out heretical. "If you bring forth what is within you, what you bring forth will save you,"[20] Jesus is supposed to have said in this Gnostic text.

In fact, Jesus' real position, spelled out in the real Gospels, was exactly the opposite: what comes out of the heart of a person is exactly what corrupts him. "For out of the heart come evil thoughts, murder, adultery, sexual immorality, theft, false testimony, slander" (Mt 15:19).

Steinem has frequently championed women who feel they have collectively suffered from a male hierarchical society. For many women who have truly been abused at the hands of fathers, husbands, or boyfriends, Steinem's words appear to conjure a new, consoling universe into which they can plunge—in effect, a new hope for their lives.

The universe, at first glance, seems to be one of self-discovery. But it is self-discovery with a price tag, namely self-worship. In the end, the universe reveals everything else it contains: pantheism, the occult, sharing your backyard with witchcraft, and embracing a view of religion that is flatly hostile to the Jewish and Christian traditions while cozily hospitable to virtually every other tradition.

In a chapter entitled "Religion versus Spirituality," Steinem makes it clear that she opposes all traditional religions, above all those that invoke an all-powerful, personal God. In their place, she advocates "an immediately experienced, universal spirituality." Movements that have undertaken this, she says, have made the point that "pagan, a word made to seem negative, really just means 'of the country' and originally signified those who believed in the divinity of all living things."[21] In an appendix, she adds a "Meditation Guide" that encourages readers to look for a "deeper, unconscious, back-of-the-mind self" that is to be the "guide" on a daily meditative journey.[22]

HUMAN POTENTIAL AND HOPE

Where does that journey lead? For Steinem, the ultimate goal is not even God in a pantheistic sense, but something that falls under the rubric of human potential, a concept of the possibilities of virtually limitless human development. Steinem has made it explicit that human potential is her ultimate hope for the human race. There are, of course, a variety of psychological and self-improvement programs marketed commercially that accept the premises of human potential. At least one of them, however, explicitly embraces the idea of self-deification as a valid part of the pursuit of the human potential hope.

*Y*ou *are the Supreme being.... "Reality" is a reflection of your notions. Totally. Perfectly.*

One such is est (Erhard Seminars Training), or as it has formally renamed itself, Forum. Those who have attended Forum training seminars are encouraged to think of themselves as being a part of every atom that exists in the world, and at the same time as comprising the sum of all other existing atoms. A graduate of est training, Carl Frederick, has written: "You are the Supreme being... 'Reality' is a reflection of your notions. Totally. Perfectly."[23]

To pursue the search for hope in the furthest development of the human potential, of course, takes men and women in a direction 180 degrees removed from the Jewish and Christian view. Clearly, the orthodox view is that men and women must never set up a false image to worship, whether of their own selves or some quite separate deity who is not the same as the God of Abraham, Isaac, and Jacob and Who revealed his law through Moses on Mount Sinai.

The deity of human potential is not at all the infinite, loving, personal

God against whom (Jews and Christians alike believe) the ancestors of the human race consciously rebelled back in the Garden of Eden. It is, in fact, the Serpent himself, the one who first offered the promise of being "like God" if men and women would try out a particular kind of forbidden knowledge. That deity uttered the first great lie in human history, one which has tormented the search for hope ever since: "Your eyes will be opened," the Serpent whispered to Eve, "and you will be like God, knowing good and evil" (Gn 3:5).

It was not a good bargain.

NEW AGE AND THE DIVINITY OF MAN

However, that bargain has also been at the center of the last of the four major sources of false hope that arose from the Hegelian revolution in European thought. It is not important whether we call it a "movement" or a "cult" or simply capitalize it to signify something easier to describe than define. New Age on one level is actually the direct, logical consequence of developing the three earlier sources to their fullest. But on another, it is the reappearance—perhaps reincarnation would be a better term—of ancient, pre-Christian belief systems central to pagan thought, witchcraft, and other nontheistic cults and religions as old as the oldest of available human records in any culture.

New Age challenges to the Christian faith were present in force at the beginning of the Christian era in the form of Gnosticism. Even when Europe and the Americas were largely Christianized, New Age beliefs continued to exist, underground, and to spring up from time to time in the form of witchcraft, fascination with the occult, with psychic phenomena, and with what Aldous Huxley termed the "Perennial Philosophy." New Age may pose as a new human stage of spirituality, but it is really the oldest system of spiritual rebellion on record, already seasoned in Old Testament times.

Its genealogy from Rationalism is relatively simple to chart. The great rebellion against Christianity in nineteenth-century Europe was led, as we saw, by Feuerbach. His ideas bore fruit in both Marx and Freud. Freud, in turn, influenced Carl Jung and those who developed the psychology of selfism. As soon as the Rationalist-based systems of thought came into existence, however, they demonstrated their limitations.

Even before selfism had run its course as a focal point of psychotherapeutic theory, many of its advocates, students, and patients had concluded that it was an imperfect system. People have always somehow understood that the self alone cannot be relied upon to solve truly serious personal problems. They may have said that they seek self-knowledge in the traditional sense of the term: the discovery and acknowledgment of one's weaknesses and strengths and the effort to adjust personal behavior and attitudes in consequence. Yet people have always known something else: that focus on the self beyond what is necessary for a healthy life quickly becomes a quest for personal power.

Everyone in the world wants hope in some sense of the term. But those who attempt to grasp hold of it by elevating themselves to godhood, or by becoming little gods, have already succumbed to the Garden of Eden temptation. To gain power for the acquisition of hope, they have directly disobeyed God's commandment against idolatry.

This is the very essence of the promise of hope offered by the New Age movement. The term, of course, covers a wide spectrum of beliefs and practices ranging from a mild dose of pantheism—the belief that God is in all things and that we are all part of God—to out-and-out occult practices like channeling, which is age-old spiritism, the search for altered consciousness through drugs, and finally witchcraft

The New Age deliberately seeks:

- To eliminate the separation between God and humanity that is fundamental to Judaism and Christianity;
- To reject any criterion of truth in comparing various world religious systems;
- To deny the existence of any independent moral absolutes applicable to human behavior in all circumstances;
- To blur all distinctions between spiritual experience in the sense of communication with a spirit world and human experience in the sense of behavior universally accepted as common to the human species (being born, falling in love, having children, and so forth).

and satanic worship. Several books have shown why New Age thinking is so inimical to Christian and indeed Jewish belief, and where the biblical world view flatly contradicts that of the New Age.[24]

In the New Age cosmology, everything operates on the same plane, and everything, in some ultimate sense, is interconnected with everything else: monism. It sounds wonderfully democratic until you realize that you and Adolf Hitler are standing in line for the same cosmological social security benefits.

THE PROMISE OF GODHOOD

Out of all this flow three very important principles of New Age thinking. The first is that there is no distinction between the human and the divine. Standing together on the same plane, there is no difference between them. The human is part of the divine and vice versa.

The second is that there is no distinction between life and death, or more concretely, between those who are alive now and those who were alive in earlier periods of time. Communication is thus presumed to be possible with people who may have been dead quite a long time but who, in the New Age concept of interconnectedness, can somehow communicate back and forth with we who are alive.

The third principle is that there is no such thing as good or evil.

We have already glanced into the man-is-divine concept in our brief digression into Gnosticism, and we have seen how the human potential movement openly advocates self-deification. What is no less disturbing, though, is how modern paganism and its first cousin, witchcraft, quite bluntly espouse the very temptation offered by the Serpent to Eve. As a New Age writer herself acknowledges, "Most would agree that the goal of Neo-Paganism is, in part, to become what we potentially are, to become 'as the gods,' or, if we are God/dess, to recognize it, to make our God-dess-hood count for something."[25]

E*ach soul is its own god. You must never worship anyone or anything other than self. For you are God.*

Movie star Shirley MacLaine, perhaps the best-known New Age celebrity, expresses it with characteristic clarity: "Each soul is its own god. You must never worship anyone or anything other than self. For you are God."[26] In fact, New Age thinking doesn't stop there. It claims to be hospitable to all varieties of religious thought. Nominally, it even includes

Christianity. In practice, it is profoundly hostile both to orthodox Judaism and to orthodox Christianity (evangelical or traditional Protestant, or committed Roman Catholic or Eastern Orthodox) precisely because neither of these beliefs will compromise the transcendence and separateness of God.

Virtually all of the New Age principles were set forth by the famous occultist of the nineteenth century we mentioned before, the Russian writer Madame Helena Blavatsky. A cofounder of the Theosophical Society in New York in 1875, Blavatsky explored every aspect of spiritist communication (channeling), esoteric knowledge, and hypnotic experience. In the process, she became not only a psychic of formidable power but a woman of encyclopedic knowledge of world religion and of the occult traditions.

In her books, some of which were clearly written down while she was in a semi-trance in a form of channeling, she expressed relentless hostility to Christianity and orthodox Judaism, but a friendly view of every other religion.[27] She enjoyed describing the Christian faith in the most blasphemous terms possible and sided with Satan in looking at the Genesis account of the fall of Adam and Eve.

"The Serpent," she wrote, not Jehovah, was "the real creator and benefactor, the Father of spiritual mankind. For it was he who opened the eyes of Adam."[28] Though she originally described herself as a Buddhist, her views helped draw together ancient Western Gnosticism, occultism, and Hindu and Buddhist philosophy. As a leading scholar on the history of Theosophy has written: "Together with the Western occult tradition, the Theosophists have provided almost all the underpinnings of the 'New Age' movement, their esoteric reflection...."[29]

One of those underpinnings, though less often commented upon in examinations of New Age thought, is the second of the principles mentioned above, the unwillingness to distinguish between life and death. As, once again, Shirley MacLaine puts it: "Birth into the physical is... a limitation of the spirit, and death of the physical is the return of the spirit to its proper domain."[30]

The elimination of distinctions between life and death has several purposes in New Age thinking. One of them is to be consistent with the overriding New Age principle of monism: Everything is interconnected. Another is to make it more attractive to everyone. After all, almost nothing in life is held in greater awe and fear by most human beings in every culture and epoch than the fact of physical death itself.

CHANNELING NEW AGE HOPE

Since traditional monotheistic religions have acquired great support from their promise to followers of life after death, under certain conditions, New Age could hardly come up with a less attractive offer. A third purpose is to pave the way for a greater openness to one of the most important aspects of all New Age thinking, namely the concept of channeling.

Channeling, very simply, is communication with the spirit world through a medium. In old-fashioned terms, it is spiritism, one of the occult practices forcefully condemned in the Old Testament (see Leviticus 19:31, Deuteronomy 18:10-12) and uniformly opposed by every single branch of orthodox Christendom throughout Christian history: Eastern Orthodox, Roman Catholic, and Protestant.

Spiritists have always claimed that they are making contact with the world of spirits who once were alive but who have passed on into other worlds (spiritists are usually quite vague as to what those worlds are). Jews and Christians, however, have always held that the spirits with whom the contact is made are not those of human beings at all but are "familiar spirits," as the Bible calls them: demons whose purpose is to deceive people about the nature of God, man, life, death, and sin.

And deceive they do. One of the best-known channelers, the late Jane Roberts, who channeled a spirit calling itself Seth, attributed to Seth these words: "In a sense there is no such thing as God, God does not exist."[31] Spirits channeled invariably assert the existence of reincarnation, the sameness of all religions, and the goodness of Jesus Christ.

What they will absolutely *never* do is agree with the Christian belief that the death of Jesus Christ was a sacrificial atonement for the sins of the world, or that the only way to God is through Jesus Christ.[32] This at least ought to evoke a certain suspicion on the part of open-minded people investigating the New Age. After all, if all religions are supposedly equal— a New Age postulate—why should the spirits who agreeably channel every other kind of thought process into New Age adherents flatly refuse to consent to the channeling of Christian beliefs?

This, though, points the way to the third principle of New Age thinking, the absence of any distinction between good and evil. At its most brazen, this viewpoint tends to be expressed most strongly by New Age proponents with strong Hindu backgrounds. As one of the most highly esteemed thinkers of the New Age tradition, Swami Vivekananda (quoted by Gloria Steinem in her book), put it: "Good and evil are one and the same," and "The murderer too, is God."[33]

He also said, "Who can say that God does not manifest Himself as Evil as well as Good? But only the Hindu dares to worship him in the evil.... How few have dared to worship death, or Kali! Let us worship death!"[34] This is not a position that some of the Hollywood celebrity New Agers may wish to publicize. After all, the movie actress Sharon Tate was murdered by a man who believed exactly what Swami Vivekananda did. Charles Manson, according to an acquaintance of the cult leader, thought that the issue of good or evil, of murdering or not murdering, simply depended on karma.[35]

But it is not just Hindu-influenced New Agers who have completely dispensed with good and evil in any moral sense. One of the most popular and influential of all New Age works is *A Course in Miracles.*[36] Allegedly, this book was channeled by Jesus to a Jewish psychologist and atheist, Helen Schucman, who claims the inspiration as "the Christ."

Schucman has Jesus explaining that evil is simply an illusion and that sin is also an illusion separating us from our own "godhood." We are back, yet again, into Gnosticism: Sin is merely ignorance, and gnosis, or channeling, or some other form of consciousness-alteration will help get us out of it, and indeed any other troubles, that we may happen to be in.

T*he New Age, in many ways, is the ultimate false hope.*

Professional magicians who perform conjuring tricks—pulling rabbits out of hats, sawing ladies in half on stage, and so forth—are often called illusionists. They give the impression of doing something that they are really not doing at all. In the search for hope, that is what every practitioner of the New Age is doing, performing an illusion by dramatically distracting the audience from what is really happening.

The New Age, in many ways, is the ultimate false hope—the cosmic dead end where human despair, demonic deception, and sheer ignorance will lead the unwary, the self-worshipers, and the power seekers. Yet, beyond all that there remains genuine hope. Outlined clearly on the bright horizon of life, once a person turns away from all false hopes, is the only worthwhile source of hope that humanity has ever been offered: He is the Messiah, Jesus Christ.

EIGHT

True Hope and the Messiah

The verdict of St. Paul on the pagan world of his day is abrupt. And if you are squeamish about peremptory judgments, it is quite harsh. "Remember that at the time you were separate from Christ," he tells the new Christian believers in Ephesus, "[you were] without hope and without God in the world" (Eph 2:12).

When it comes to the matter of death, he tells the Thessalonians, they shouldn't grieve "like the rest of men, who have no hope" (1 Thes 4:13).

For Paul, it is simply a self-evident truth that the pagan world of the first century A.D. was a philosophical morass of cynicism and despair. Even at the very height of Greek civilization, the Greeks themselves were at best ambivalent, at worst quite dubious about the value of any kind of hope.

"THAT WE MIGHT HAVE HOPE..."

Paul, though, even toward the end of an amazingly adventurous life in the service of the gospel, a life often clouded by discouragement and persecution, boldly proclaims his conviction of the purpose of God's past and present message to the Israelites. It can, quite simply, be summed up as hope. He says: "For everything that was written in the past was written to teach us, so that through endurance and the encouragement of the Scriptures, we might have hope."

Is it fair to say that hope is the central theme of the Messianic promise, the essence of the message of Jesus Christ? Absolutely. In his Letter to the Colossians, Paul flatly states that the Christian hope is the sustaining essence of what Christians believe about life as a whole. To allow the life of Christ to shine through himself, Paul tells the Colossians, is to make known to the Gentiles, that is, to the pagan world of his day, "the glorious riches of this mystery, which is Christ in you, the hope of glory" (Col 1:27).

> # G*od is man's hope; therefore, man hopes in God.*

The good news of the gospel is not simply about forgiveness for sins and escape from the wrath of God. It is about connecting believers with something absolutely extraordinary that God has prepared for them in the future. It is about the glory of having within oneself the source of all truth, all love, all holiness, all righteousness, all forgiveness, and all healing—the Messiah himself.

Hope, quite simply, is the thread that links believers to Jesus Christ in the present and to the "riches of glory" in the future. As one commentary puts it, "Hope links together the two parties of the covenant: God is man's hope; therefore, man hopes in God. Hope is intricately involved in the total matter of divine action and human response."[1]

Why was Paul, a Jew of the tribe of Benjamin, a strict Pharisee and legalist, so hounded by the religious leaders of the day that they tried to kill him? It was, quite simply, because he had introduced a wholly new idea into the philosophy of the age. He offered a hope based upon a new relationship with God through the Messiah. Paul himself put it to his accusers when he was asked to explain his views to King Agrippa and Queen Bernice while under arrest at Caesarea: "It is because of my hope in what God has promised our fathers that I am on trial today" (Acts 26:6). Months later, after surviving a harrowing trip to Rome in chains, he says almost exactly the same thing to the leaders of the Jewish community there: "It is because of the hope of Israel that I am bound with this chain" (Acts 28:20).

JESUS—MESSIANIC HOPE FULFILLED

Hope simply explodes from the pages of the New Testament. At one level, the reason is obvious: Jesus himself is the promised "hope of Israel," the Messiah to whose coming the Jews looked with increasing longing, especially after the trauma of their Babylonian exile and present occupation by Rome. In the Gospel of Matthew, the apostle makes this quite explicit, citing the Messianic prophecy from Isaiah 42:1-4 and clearly identifying Jesus with it: "Here is my servant whom I have chosen, the one I love, in whom I delight; I will put my Spirit on him and he will proclaim justice to the nations.... In his name, the nations will put their hope" (Mt 12:18, 21).

The primary hope of the gospel, therefore, is the identification of the Messianic promise of the Old Testament with Jesus of Nazareth. As we've already noted, the prophetic Scriptures in the Bible increasingly looked to Israel's hope in messianic terms.

Yet the hope offered by the New Testament is based on more than—wonderful though it is—the announcement of the Messianic incarnation in Jesus. It actually arises from the deliberate contrast that Paul and the other apostles draw between the remoteness of the Old Testament concept of hope and the intimacy of the hope that can be lived out in the lives of the new community of believers once they have acknowledged the lordship of Jesus Christ.

In the Letter to the Hebrews, for example, the writer (probably not Paul, in the consensus of most scholars) reminds his Jewish audience that the promises God made to Abraham were made before the introduction of the Law through Moses on Mount Sinai. They were made, he insists, quite independently of the requirements of the Law to be given by Moses, because the Law was announced from Mount Sinai centuries after Abraham was already dead.

In view of this discrepancy in time between the promises of God on the one hand and the commandments of God on the other, he argues, how could the Jewish Law, the Old Covenant, ever be considered the means through which the Jews were to receive the blessings and promises God had made to them? "If perfection could have been obtained through the Levitical priesthood," the writer asks, "(for on the basis of it the law was given to the people), why was there still need for another priest to come, one in the order of Melchizedek, not in the order of Aaron?" (Heb 7:11).

This is the key question in our search for understanding about the nature of the New Testament hope. The need for a new high priest, the Hebrews author explains in his magnificent exposition of what faith and hope are all about, occurred because the Law—the Old Covenant—simply was not capable of making men and women morally perfect. Now, though, that possibility, asserts our author, incredible though it may seem, has been made available.

"The former regulation," he says triumphantly, "is set aside because it was weak and useless (for the law made nothing perfect), and a *better* hope is introduced, by which we draw near to God" (Heb 7:18-19, italics ours). The "better hope," simply, is access for all believers in Jesus to the "Most Holy Place" (in some biblical translations also called the "Holy of Holies") that the Jewish High Priest, under the terms of the Old Covenant, was able to enter only once a year.

In the Old Testament, the "Most Holy Place" was physically the innermost part of the Jewish Temple in Jerusalem that was separated from the rest of the Temple chamber by a curtain. The curtain denoted symbolically the unapproachability of God. In the New Testament account of the crucifixion, however, we are told that, at the very moment of the death of Jesus on the cross, the curtain "was torn in two from top to bottom" (Mt 27:51). The event, we must assume, was as literal as the crucifixion itself. Yet it also symbolized dramatically that the death of Jesus had broken down the curtain of unapproachability between worshipers of God and God himself.

As the writer of Hebrews continues, the access to the presence of God that has now been obtained through the one-time sacrifice of Jesus (instead of the Old Testament sacrifice by the High Priest once a year) has now become so real that we can enter it, awe-inspiring though it is, with complete confidence. In his words, we can gain access "in full assurance of faith" (Heb 10:22). This incredible access to God's mercy and grace is now quite simply "the hope we profess," which we must "hold unswervingly to" (Heb 10:23). The word hold is not used idly. In the Letter to the Hebrews, this hope is described in such concrete terms that it is nothing less than "an anchor for the soul, firm and secure" (Heb 6:19), the very foundation upon which a mature Christian life is to be built.

REVOLUTIONARY NEW TESTAMENT HOPE

There are actually a total of eighty-five occurrences of the English word *hope* as verb (with its various endings) or noun in the New International Version of the New Testament.[2] Almost every single occurrence of the English *hope* is a translation of either the noun *elpis* (English transliteration), which means "hope," or the verb *elpizo*, which means "I hope." *Elpis* was a common enough word in classical Greek, but it started its career in pre-Christian times as an almost neutral idea. A hope could be good or bad.

E lpis *means "hope." The verb* elpizo *means "I hope."*

In a way hope was little more than a wish, corresponding today very much to the use of the word in our largely post-Christian world as in, "I hope it doesn't rain today." If we paraphrase this perfectly ordinary sentence, what we really get is this: "It is my desire that there be no rain today, but I fully understand that my desire may have little to do with what the weather actually does." In short, if this is the nature of your hope, you'd better carry an umbrella with you, figuratively and literally, most of the time.

New Testament times, of course, in many respects presented people with dilemmas about life's decisions identical to those of our own era. They may not have had umbrellas in the first century A.D., but they knew all about the same, soggy hopes. In the New Testament, there are several occurrences of this "modern" usage of the noun *elpis* or the verb *elpizo*. For example, when Herod has an opportunity to meet with Jesus after his arrest in the Garden of Gethsamene, the Gospel of Luke tells us that Herod "hoped to see him perform some miracle" (Lk 23:8).

The Apostle Paul, though a magnificent explainer of what the New Testament hope really means, had some entirely down-to-earth hopes (desires) of his own. "I plan to visit you when I go to Spain," Paul told the Christians in Rome. "I hope to visit you while passing through and to have you assist me on my journey there" (Rom 15:24).

"I hope in the Lord Jesus to send Timothy to you soon," he told the Philippians, "that I also may be cheered when I receive news about you" (Phil 2:19). There is nothing theological about these expressions. They are thoroughly human.

What, then, is so special about the hope that the New Testament introduces to the whole human race? First, let's look at some interesting facts about the usage of the word. It is never used as an adverbial form as, for example, in the common English expression "hopefully." It is found, in any variety of *elpis* or *elpizo*, only in five places in the Gospels. Of these five occurrences, it is clear that in two of them the meaning corresponds exactly to hope as "trust," which we saw so much in the Old Testament.

One of those occurrences is the Matthew 12:21 reference, introduced earlier in this chapter: "In his name, the nations will put their hope." The other is John 5:45, where Jesus plainly employs hope in the sense of "counting on." He tells the Jewish leaders: "But do not think I will accuse you before the Father. Your accuser is Moses, on whom your hopes are set." In the other three New Testament instances, hope is employed in its workaday meaning of desire without much conviction of fulfillment. Interestingly, and for reasons we will explain later, the word *elpis* occurs not a single time in the book of Revelation.

What then is it about the Christian hope that is so revolutionary in the New Testament?

The revolutionary nature of the New Testament hope is its power to change the way ordinary people live their lives. We saw how Paul referred to it as "an anchor for the soul." But when hope is explained fully throughout the letters of the New Testament, we find it taking on all kinds of solid-sounding attributes. In 1 Thessalonians 5:8, "the hope of salvation" is a "helmet," protecting the believer in conjunction with the other armaments of spiritual warfare, the "breastplate" of love and faith.

In that most famous scriptural passage about spiritual warfare, Ephesians 6:10-17, the "helmet of salvation" is the piece of armor that protects the head (the seat of the mind) whereas the "breastplate of righteousness" protects the heart (the seat of the will and the emotions).

What does this tell us about hope?

It suggests that whereas both righteousness and faith, represented by a shield in the Ephesians passage, are items of spiritual protection closely connected to the will and the emotions, the Christian concept of hope is firmly connected to the mind. Hope is not at all an emotion in the Christian sense. It is not desire or wish. More than anything else, it is expectation.

HOPE AND EXPECTATION

When I board a plane from New York to San Francisco to spend Christmas with my wife's sister and her family, I "expect" to arrive after a flight of a few hours. If my wife and I told her sister and the sister's husband that I "hope" to get there after a few hours' flight, there might be some concern in my sister-in-law's home. What might go wrong on the journey? Is the plane one of those commuter aircraft whose safety record has sometimes been questioned? Might I be detained—who knows, even robbed or kidnapped—on the way to the airport? This kind of hope is obviously not expectation at all.

Yet our New Testament hope is both confident expectation and something more as well. "Our hope [expectation] for you is firm," Paul explains to the Corinthians, despite the problems they have had in their church, "because we know that just as you share in our sufferings, so also you share in our comfort" (2 Cor 1:7).

Yet in Philippians, Paul says, "I eagerly expect and hope that I will in no way be ashamed, but will have sufficient courage that now as always Christ will be exalted in my body, whether by life or by death" (Phil 1:20). Now if I "expect" to arrive in San Francisco a few hours after leaving Washington, what does my mere "hope" to do so amount to? Plainly, not very much.

But the hope introduced by the New Testament is very much a vigorous looking forward to, a sense of warm anticipation quite different from uncertainty over the plane ride that *hope* might otherwise mean. In fact, perhaps the closest translation of the use of *hope* in the New Testament is indeed "definite looking forward to." This is well illustrated by Paul's comment in Galatians, "But by faith we eagerly await through the Spirit the righteousness for which we hope" (Gal 5:5). Here, *eagerly await* is synonymous with *hope*.

One of the most famous passages in the entire New Testament is the beginning of Hebrews 11, where we read, "Now faith is being sure of what we hope for and certain of what we do not see" (Heb 11:1). In other words, faith and hope are not only intimately connected, but they tell us something about the sequence of how we relate to God and how we go about our prayers.

There are plenty of religions where people pray with great faith, if faith means a zealous desire that the deity should grant a certain wish. What the New Testament makes clear, though, is that our hope—our confident expectation of how God will order things—is the foundation on which we operate our faith.

Nowhere is this more dramatically illustrated than in Paul's Letter to the Corinthians, "If only for this life we have hope in Christ, we are to be pitied more than all men" (1 Cor 15:19). Why pitied? Because, Paul explains, the basis of what we pray for in our mundane daily existence is not a God whose kingdom is limited to the here and now. After all, a religion whose founder was asserted to be divine but who couldn't do anything for you when you died wouldn't be worth much. That is what Paul seems to be saying in this passage.

The Christian hope for the future has both a present and future reality. It is present because it starts from the moment we ally our lives with Christ and allow him to direct us in building the Kingdom of God. It is future because our expectation of God's goodness to us stretches into the infinite spaces of eternity. Far from being a pie-in-the-sky notion, this new Christian hope is utterly concrete in how it affects us, so concrete that Paul encourages us to become well acquainted with it, as one might become acquainted with a friend, with a horse one rides, or with a house one has bought.

He writes, "I pray also that the eyes of your heart may be enlightened in order that you may *know* the hope to which he has called you, the riches of his glorious inheritance in the saints, and his incomparably great power for us who believe" (Eph 1:18-19, italics added).

Hope is solid enough for faith and knowledge actually to rest on it (Ti 1:1-2), for us to hold on to it and boast about it (Heb 3:6), to profess it (Heb 10:23), to be joyful in it (Rom 12:12), and to be able to explain it quite specifically when we are asked about our faith (1 Pt 3:15). Hope is so radical an innovation in human thought that the Christian concept of it almost explodes at us out of the New Testament.

A LIVING HOPE

The most hope-filled letter is not by Paul but by the Apostle Peter. His first letter has sometimes been called "a letter of hope" because hope is a recurrent theme within it. There are five ringing references to hope in this brief letter:

> Praise be to the God and Father of our Lord Jesus Christ! In his great mercy he has given us new birth into a living hope through the resurrection of Jesus Christ from the dead, and into an inheritance that can never perish, spoil or fade—kept in heaven for you, who through faith are shielded by God's power until the coming of the salvation that is ready to be revealed in the last time. **1 Peter 1:5-6**

Therefore, prepare your minds for action; be self-controlled; set your hope fully on the grace to be given you when Jesus Christ is revealed.

1 Peter 1:13

Through him you believe in God, who raised him from the dead and glorified him, so that your faith and hope are in God.   **1 Peter 1:21**

For this is the way the holy women of the past who put their hope in God used to make themselves beautiful.   **1 Peter 3:5**

But in your hearts set apart Christ as Lord. Always be prepared to given an answer to everyone who asks you to give the reason for the hope that you have.   **1 Peter 3:15**

The first question that immediately arises from these verses is simply, what does Peter mean by a hope that is living? One thing is obvious. Whatever else *living* means, no one can acquire it without entering into the new birth: a unique, God-given relationship with the Father in heaven. Peter makes it clear that the new, "living hope" of which he speaks derives directly from the new relationship with God through Jesus that has been made available to everyone who wants it through the death and resurrection of the Messiah himself.

> *The living hope arises from a living relationship with Jesus Christ, a spiritual connection between people and God, mediated only through Jesus, unattainable through any other religion or faith system.*

The living hope arises from a living relationship with Jesus Christ, a spiritual connection between people and God, mediated only through Jesus, unattainable through any other religion or faith system. This living hope is certainly not something one can find at the supermarket. At the same time, once this spiritual connection has been made—through a person consciously deciding to commit his or her life to Jesus Christ—the New Testament hope comes alive for that individual.

A HOPE THAT NEVER FADES AWAY

By definition, this hope never fades away, and it is intended to play a vital role in how a person lives his or her Christian life. What it does is this: It connects our entire circumstances and condition in the present with what God has planned for us when we finally come into his presence in heaven. The New Testament hope is thus a kind of golden thread linking our present, however difficult it may be, with an incredibly wonderful future that has been guaranteed us. It is the inward assurance that everything the Lord has promised to those who follow him will come to pass and the spiritual conviction necessary to put our faith to work along the way.

The way we acquire this hope is by asking the Holy Spirit to make it real in our lives. In Romans 15:13 Paul prays, "May the God of hope fill you with all joy and peace as you trust in him, so that you may overflow with hope by the power of the Holy Spirit."

Paul obviously understands hope as a condition in the life of a believer that has a profound impact on the way he or she believes. For the Christian, the living hope spoken of by the Apostle Peter infects the whole of our lives in this positive fashion, both our natural lives and our spiritual lives.

It's important to understand something else about hope before we go any further. Hope in many ways is paradoxical: It insists on saying "yes" about things when circumstances are shouting "no." In Romans, Paul reminds us of the story of Abraham, who did something that his contemporaries must have considered quite ridiculous.

A successful and wealthy land and livestock owner, Abraham abandoned everything to follow God's calling upon him into the land of Canaan. He even believed that God could somehow produce a child from the womb of his wife, even though she was already long past childbearing age, since God had promised to do so. Paul's purpose in referring to Abraham is to explain the entire notion of justification by faith rather than by works. But it is striking that, when he comes to describing the radical nature of Abraham's obedience and faith in God, he writes simply: "Against all hope, Abraham in hope believed and so became the father of many nations, just as it had been said to him, 'So shall your offspring be'" (Rom 4:18).

In the human sense, there were no longer any grounds for hope for Abraham. When he believed God, he did so by refusing to accept the limits imposed on reason and the emotions by human hope. He thus believed "against all hope." In an important sense, therefore, just as Abraham is a model for the exercise of faith, he also demonstrates how to exercise hope.

HOPE—AN ACT OF THE WILL

Did Abraham understand hope in the New Testament sense that we have been explaining? Probably not, at least at the outset of his faith walk with God. What Paul is saying, though, is that Abraham's exercise of faith was also an exercise of hope, a demonstration even before hope was fully understood, that the New Testament hope is not an emotion but an act of will.

An act of will? How can that be? How can hope be set in motion by the will? It can be done the same way that faith is set in motion by the will, not as the result of some gooey sentiment, some declarative, rote statement of faith, but as an active decision to orient the heart to trust that God will do what he says he will do.

It is striking, in fact, that when Paul in his First Letter to Timothy describes the process of putting one's hope in something, he uses the Greek aorist tense. The aorist is used to signify a decisive action that has been started and completed and is now in the past. One would use the aorist to say "I mailed the letter yesterday." When Pontius Pilate replies to the Jewish leaders who complain about the sign he ordered attached to the cross of Jesus, "Jesus of Nazareth, King of the Jews," he uses the aorist to respond: "What I have written I have written" (in Greek, *ho gegrafa gegrafa*).

In the First Letter to Timothy, Paul refers first to himself and his companions as having put (decisively, and in the past) "[their] hope in the living God" (1 Tm 4:10). Similarly in the same letter, when he is referring to widows who deserve the charitable assistance of the church, Paul speaks of "the widow who is really in need and left all alone [and who] puts her hope in God and continues night and day to pray and to ask God for help" (1 Tm 5:5).

The NIV translation's use of *puts* does not accurately translate the Greek. The actual text says *ilpikamen,* which refers to something the widow has done and completed, not something she is in the process of doing. A literal translation would be "the widow who is really in need and left all alone and has [decisively] put her hope in God..." Hope, therefore, is something one puts into effect, exercises, practices, in precisely the same way that one exercises faith.

FAITH, HOPE, AND LOVE

What, then, is the difference between faith and hope? For many people, they seem hardly distinguishable. After all, doesn't the Old Testament employ the Hebrew words translated by the English word *hope* almost synonymously with other words translated as *faith*? Even in the New Testament the verb *hope* is used in a way that could be interchangeable with *believe* or *put faith in*. Thus in Ephesians, Paul speaks of himself and other believers as those "who were the first to hope in Christ" (Eph 1:11-12).

But hope and faith are not the same at all. Along with love, they comprise what have been described over the years as "the theological virtues." The function of these virtues is to turn people toward God; they have God as their object, as opposed to the moral virtues or fruits of the Spirit.

"Faith," the author of the Letter to the Hebrews writes, "is being sure of what we hope for and certain of what we do not see" (Heb 11:1). As one writer has put it, "The hope which is set before men produces and vindicates the faith by which they seize it."[3]

Faith is an act of will initiated by the heart, or it might be said, an act of trust. It is well illustrated by the perhaps apocryphal story of the famous French tightrope walker Blondin (1824-1897), who is reported to have asked an awed audience whether any one of them thought he could walk a tightrope across the Niagara Falls carrying a wheelbarrow (he did in fact cross the Niagara Falls that way several times, and on one occasion actually with a wheelbarrow).

A nice little old lady said, yes, she thought he could do that.

"Thank you," Blondin replied. "And do you think I could accomplish this while carrying someone in the barrow?"

"Oh yes," said the admiring lady.

"Very well," replied the famous Frenchman with a twinkle in his eyes. "Would you like to be the passenger in the wheelbarrow?"

The lady was silent. She had hope in Blondin's future accomplishments but not the personal faith to trust him to accomplish them.

In the case of both faith and hope, there is an act of will involved that embraces both the heart and the mind—faith requiring more of the heart, and hope more of the mind. Faith seems to operate more in the area of action, of stepping out and doing. Hope seems to belong more to the realm of imagination, of seeing with the mind's eye what is not visible to the real eye.

Paul, in his Letter to the Romans, puts it this way: "For in this hope [act of definite looking forward to] we were saved. But hope that is seen is no hope at all. Who hopes for what he already has? But if we hope for what we do not yet have, we wait for it patiently" (Rom 8:24-25). Faith, by contrast, was "being sure of what we hope for." Hope, so to speak, has set up in the mind's eye the wonderful promise of God's future action, and faith is what propels the believer to act out that hope in daily life.

The reason that faith, hope, and love are mentioned together as the theological virtues is that they often are linked together in the New Testament as foundational to living a mature Christian life. In the most famous New Testament passage on love, 1 Corinthians 13, Paul sums up his magnificent description of the qualities of Christian love (*agape* in Greek, a fruit of the spirit that is quite separate from *eros*, sexual love, or *philia*, parental, sibling, or friendship affection) by concluding, "And now these three remain: faith, hope, and love. But the greatest of these is love" (1 Cor 13:13). Their linkage is designed to produce the most fruitful of possible responses in the lives of believers.

THE PURPOSE OF CHRISTIAN HOPE

In Romans 5, Paul describes one of the fruits of faith as "peace with God," and one of the fruits of hope as joy (he actually says "we rejoice" [Rom 5:2]). In the First Letter to the Thessalonians, Paul speaks warmly of the fine responses in the lives of the Thessalonian Christians. "We continually remember before our God and Father," he says, "your work produced by faith, your labor prompted by love, and your endurance inspired by hope in our Lord Jesus Christ" (1 Thes 1:3).

Here lies the purpose of Christian hope. It is not just to make people feel joyful, though that is what it indeed does. It is to provide the Christian with spiritual muscles that can be applied to the operation not just of the other "theological virtues" of faith and love but of every aspect of the Christian life. Let's look at this more closely.

There is a wonderful reciprocal relationship among hope, faith, and love, and between these three theological virtues and the nine fruits of the Holy Spirit mentioned by Paul in his Letter to the Galatians. Those fruits—which should gradually manifest themselves in every Christian as he or she increasingly gives over his or her life to Christ—are as follows: love, joy, peace, patience, kindness, goodness, faithfulness, gentleness, and self-control (Gal 5:22-23).

What hope seems to do, when exercised, is at one level strengthen the quality of the other two virtues, faith and love. At another level hope contributes both to the fruits of the Spirit and to other desirable attributes of the Christian life. As Paul explains, hope brings forth joy (Rom 5:2), immense confidence (Rom 5:4), boldness (2 Cor 3:12), freedom (Rom 8:21), peace (Rom 5:1-3), and purity (1 Jn 3:3).

Hope in fact anticipates the righteousness of God, which we know can come only from faith. Yet as Paul indicates, just as God himself is the ultimate source of all hope, we begin to overflow with hope as we grow in joy and peace in our relationship with him: "May the God of hope fill you with all joy and peace as you trust in him, so that you may overflow with hope by the power of the Holy Spirit" (Rom 15:13).

HOPE AND JOY

There is an important connection between hope and joy, as we have already seen. But that connection seems especially important in the way Christians are called on to cope with suffering. Perhaps one of the most remarkable paradoxes of the Christian walk is that, just as hope produces the fruits of Christian character, so the development of character itself leads to the phenomenon of hope.

Paul makes this clear in Romans. "And we rejoice in the hope of the glory of God," he says. "Not only so, but we also rejoice in our sufferings, because we know that suffering produces perseverance; perseverance, character; and character, hope" (Rom 5:2-4). In other words, when things go wrong, we can be absolutely sure that the end result for us (if we don't cave in at first sight of a problem) is that our hope for the future in Christ will be even greater than it was at the beginning.

This is no doubt why the letters of Paul are full of seemingly irrational advice. "Give thanks in all circumstances, for this is God's will for you in Christ Jesus," we read in 1 Thessalonians (5:18), or "Rejoice in the Lord always. I will say it again; rejoice!" (Phil 4:4).

How can anyone give thanks when a tragedy has befallen a loved one or a family member, or even if something less catastrophic but especially annoying has happened: the car has broken down, or an unexpected bill has arrived? The answer in the New Testament is not at all to wallow in masochistic misery, which is how the passages in question might be caricatured. Rather, the spiritual and personal character that is formed in a person who does not collapse when everything seems to be going wrong, but offers up praise in an attitude of trust that God knows what is happening. This literally leads to a great welling up of joy and hope in God's mercy and grace.[4]

In a very important sense, this new joy and hope is an ultimate hope, a hope whose fulfillment cannot in the final sense take place until the return of Jesus Christ.

> For hope is not concerned with the realization of a human dream of the future but with the confidence which, directed away from the world to God, waits patiently for God's gift, and when it is received does not rest in possession, but in the assurance that God will maintain what He has given. Even in the consummation, Christian experience, in accordance with the concept of God, is inconceivable without *elpis* [hope]....The paradox that Christian hope [elpis] is itself an eschatological blessing because it sees that the Old Testament hope is fulfilled in the mission of Jesus appears most clearly in Matt 12:21 [which cites Isaiah 42:4, "in his name the nations will put their hope"].[5]

HOPE AND REVELATION

This leads to the final important observation about the occurrence of the word *hope* in the New Testament: its complete absence from the book of Revelation written by the Apostle John. The word *elpis* does not appear even once in this last book of the Bible, nor does any form of the verb *elpizo*. In its place, though, is the word *hupomone*, which is translated most commonly as "patience, endurance, perseverance."

Thus we find the resurrected Christ, in his appearance to John in the vision on the Isle of Patmos, saying to the church at Ephesus, "I know your deeds, your hard work, and your perseverance [*hupomone*]" (Rv 2:2). This message is for the church at Thyatira: "I know your deeds, your love and faith, your service and perseverance, and that you are now doing more than you did at first" (Rv 2:19).

It's important to understand that the context of the messages of the resurrected Christ to the churches of Asia was that of persecution. The severe Neronian persecution of A.D. 64 had led to the deaths of Peter and Paul, as well as many Christians in Rome. In Revelation, Christ himself was speaking to churches to encourage them during times of severe testing, especially from external forces.

Patience, endurance, and perseverance are invariably character traits that are needed during times of great pressure and persecution. We already know from the Letter to the Romans that there is a straight-line link connecting suffering, perseverance, character, and hope (5:3-5), so the resurrected Jesus did not need to spell out the fruit of perseverance and character.

The word *hope* is not present in Revelation, however, principally because the Messiah himself is present. Hope was almost absent from the Gospels for the same reason. Jesus Christ, the Alpha and the Omega, is present in Revelation, both "the God of hope" (Rom 15:13), "the hope of Israel" (Acts 28:20), "the blessed hope," as Titus describes the antici-pated appearing of Christ (Ti 2:12-14), and simply and powerfully, "our hope" (1 Tm 1:1-2).

The Christian hope, *elpis,* is already the reason that the believers of the churches of Asia are undergoing persecution. It is their hope in Christ that has caused them to be singled out for pressure from the Roman authorities. Thus, as one scholar has put it:

> Christian hope rests on the divine act of salvation accomplished in Christ, and since this is eschatalogical, hope itself is an eschatalogical blessing, i.e., now is the time when we may have confidence.[6]

So too, in the book of Revelation, the relationship of the Messiah to his people is full of hope. He is the Alpha and Omega, the victorious King who promises full participation in his sovereignty to those who conquer. This promise elicits a loyalty which takes the form of keen expectancy, continual wakefulness, and unwearying patience. Thus throughout the Bible the thought of hope fuses together the reality of God as the source and goal of expectation and the totality of faith's response: trust, eagerness, patient endurance, and joyful assurance.[7]

It would be hard to sum up more succinctly just how Revelation brings together the Messianic hope, the Messiah, and the role of hope in extending the boundaries of God's kingdom. Revelation, though the last book of canonical Scripture, nevertheless marks only the beginning of the unfolding of the understanding of hope among Christians of all epochs. How appropriate it is that the very last words of Revelation, and indeed, of all of Scripture, are the ultimate cry of hope: "Amen! Come, Lord Jesus! The grace of the Lord Jesus be with God's people. Amen" (Rv 22:20-21).

NINE

Hope and the Christian Mystery

"I will not leave you as orphans," Jesus told his disciples during his final supper with them the day before the crucifixion, "I will come to you" (Jn 14:18). These words were spoken just before what must have struck the twelve as the ultimate tragedy of Jesus' entire three-year ministry. Here was the man they believed to be the Messiah, on the point of arrest—on the point, in fact, of throwing away everything he had appeared to be working for during his three-year ministry. Yet somehow he was promising never to desert his followers. How could anything he said soften the greatest anguish they had ever experienced in their lives?

HOPE AND THE DISCIPLES

It is hard to imagine many instances of emotional horror worse than what the disciples experienced between the moment of Jesus' betrayal by Judas in the Garden of Gethsemane and the momentous discovery of his resurrection. Had Jesus not dashed their hopes? During his three years of ministry before the finale of his life in Jerusalem, Jesus had progressively demonstrated that he was not a prophet but, as the disciples slowly came to understand, the Messiah himself. He had warned them of his forthcoming execution, and they had preferred to ignore the warning.

For them, the Messiah was to be the "hope of Israel," the Redeemer who would put everything right in the benighted life of the Jewish people. But as the Roman legionaries mocked Jesus with a blindfold and blows to his face and body, gambling with dice for his seamless outer garment, what had become of their hope? Where was the hope of Israel now?

During the forty days before his ascension, Jesus repeatedly appeared to his disciples, spoke with them, answered their questions, and confirmed over and over the truth of all of his earlier teachings. By the time he disappeared from their eyes in a cloud on the Mount of Olives, Jesus had not only established himself in their eyes as the hope of Israel but he had given them a word of assurance that has echoed down through the centuries to the countless multitudes of followers of Christ on every continent of the earth: "You will receive power when the Holy Spirit comes on you," Jesus promised, "and you will be my witnesses in Jerusalem, and in all Judea and Samaria, and to the ends of the earth" (Acts 1:8).

That promise is a central part of the Christian hope. Not "you may be" or "you ought to try to be," but simply "you will be." After we receive the Holy Spirit as the disciples did, it becomes part of our nature to be witnesses. We don't even have to try. The hope for the rest of our lives, after committing ourselves to Jesus, lies in his promise.

Peter, who was second closest to Jesus after John, devoted much of one of his letters to elaborating what it meant to be witness and to hope. He wrote as the first Christian communities sprung up, just as Jesus had promised, in Judea, Samaria, and far beyond. "Set your hope fully on the grace to be given you when Jesus Christ is revealed," he told his readers in his first letter (1 Pt 1:13). "Always be prepared," he added, "to give an answer to everyone who asks you to give the reason for the hope that you have" (1 Pt 3:15).

Peter had studied Jesus intensely in the three years he had come to know him. Although Peter was not given the title "the disciple whom Jesus loved"—that was given to the profoundly thoughtful disciple, John—Peter had been the first to call Jesus the Messiah, the first to betray him, the first to be forgiven for that betrayal. Peter, who always wanted a Messiah who was a man of action, grasped exactly what it meant to have recognized, followed, and obeyed the one whom the Old Testament called the hope of Israel. No wonder Peter's first letter is sometimes called "the epistle of hope."

POST-APOSTOLIC HOPE

But what have Christians said about hope since the end of the apostolic age? Did hope become something quite theoretical because the person who embodied the Old Testament promise, Jesus, was no longer physically present to exemplify it?

By no means. Hope has intrigued and inspired generation after generation of Christians, both as something unique to the entire experience of being a Christian and as a contrast to the flimsy content of purely secular or worldly hope. It is true that, compared with the entire libraries that have been written on the other two Christian theological virtues, love and faith, the literature on hope is relatively modest. Yet in at least one period of Christian history, hope dominated the theology and Christian thinking of several generations of believers.

The symbology of the very earliest Christian drawings and art, often of a rather simple kind, scratched into the stone walls of catacombs, includes suggestive hints that the concept of hope was extremely important for the earliest Christian converts from paganism. There is often a drawing of an anchor. The upper part of the drawing, with the cross-bar and the central shaft, of course, forms a cross. Those early Christians must also have been familiar with Paul's description of hope as "anchor for the soul" (Heb 6:19).

In the writings of the early Church Fathers in the decades immediately following the apostolic age, there are frequent references to hope. In the First Letter of Clement, written about A.D. 96, the author, who was the third bishop of Rome, writes earnestly to the Corinthian church to urge them not to depart from true Christian doctrine in favor of an elitist understanding of spiritual experience that may have had connections with ancient Gnostic heresies.

Speaking with vigor about the reality of the physical resurrection of the dead and referring to Old Testament texts that speak of this (see Job 19:26), Clement boldly asserts, "With this hope, then, let us attach ourselves to him who is faithful to his promises and just in his judgments."[1] At another point, he implores those causing dissension in the Corinthian church to "reflect upon the common nature of our hope."[2]

This use of the word *hope* was not a chance incident. The following century, the Christian philosopher Athenagoras, writing in Greek and living in Alexandria, addressed an appeal to the Roman Emperor, Marcus Aurelius, asking him to ignore false accusations that the Christian faith was atheistic (because it denied the real existence of the deities of paganism), a cover for incest (a reference to the tendency of early Christians to refer to their fellowship as a brotherhood), or even cannibalistic (an obvious misreading of the early church's practice of holy communion on each occasion that it met). After dismissing the charges of incest ("We think of some as sons and daughters. Others we regard as brothers and sisters."), Athenagoras asserts boldly, "Having, therefore, the hope of eternal life, we despise the enjoyments of the present, even the pleasures of the soul."[3]

W*ith this hope, then, let us attach ourselves to him who is faithful to his promises and just in his judgments.*

But it was St. Augustine (354-430), that polymath of spiritual and literary knowledge, who laid the foundations of much of the later elaboration of the meaning of Christian hope. Augustine made it clear that Christian hope was quite different from that of pagans. "You do not hope as the gentiles hope," he wrote in one of his sermons. "They hope for the vanities of secular life, you for eternal life with Christ."[4] He added in another place, "In Christ the believer already has the thing in which he hopes."[5]

Augustine, in addition to discussing the two great enemies of true hope, despair and presumption, perceptively noted that the possession of true hope was dependent upon at least one important attitude of the heart on the part of the one hoping, namely humility.[6] He did not formulate a systematic study of the theological virtue of hope, but he pointed toward its outline.

ST. THOMAS AQUINAS AND HOPE

Such a study was made, however, by St. Thomas Aquinas (1225-1274), whose relentless examination of the virtue of hope in almost all of its conceivable occurrences (in heaven, on earth, in the life of Jesus, etc.) almost completely exhausts the topic. Aquinas speculates whether hope exists in "the irascible appetite" (as a purely human desire) and concludes that this is not true hope. He also comes to the conclusion that hope will not exist in heaven because the saint will already possess that which, while he or she is a pilgrim in the walk of faith on earth, he or she can only hope for.[7]

Aquinas has a useful definition of the difference between faith, on the one side, and presumption and despair on the other. Presumption, argues Aquinas, consists in expecting God to deliver to the Christian blessings or answers to prayer regardless of a person's godliness. Despair, by contrast, is the sin of not expecting from God the blessings and grace that a godly Christian would be entitled to ask for. Aquinas concludes: "But there can be no excess of hope in comparison with God, Whose goodness is infinite."[8]

For all of his rather tedious hair-splitting, Aquinas nevertheless made three major contributions to understanding how hope works in the life of a believer. First, he grasped that the Christian hope was a God-originated quality, the product of what is called grace.

Second, he stressed that, by entering into the very presence of God after the resurrection, Christ has anchored our hope in heaven itself. "Christ has entered for us into the inner sanctuary of the tent [the Old Testament Tabernacle], and has made firm our hope."[9] The Latin term Aquinas uses for "made firm" is *fixit*, the past tense of the verb *fingere*, to attach. But I prefer to think of the English-language connotation of "fixed it," which sounds like "fixit." Christ has "fixed" our hope to a solid point in heaven itself, from which nothing can uproot it.

> *Christ has "fixed" our hope to a solid point in heaven itself, from which nothing can uproot it.*

Third, and perhaps most important, Aquinas introduced the idea that hope was the great virtue of the Christian as a wayfarer through life. The Latin term Aquinas used was *viator*, or wayfarer, an idea that was taken up (and almost certainly not copied) by the great seventeenth-century English Puritan writer Bunyan in his *Pilgrim's Progress*.

The *viator*, or wayfarer, of Aquinas, as prominent twentieth-century writer on hope Josef Pieper has said, is "one journeying toward eternal life."[10] In this sense, one who walks in the Christian hope must also certainly be a person who has faith. Pieper adds, "If one does not believe in the God of the Christians, he cannot hope in Him.... The first step toward God must be by faith."[11]

The relentless, system-building mind of Aquinas may have subjected hope to unnecessary speculative examination, but not even Aquinas was able to squelch the irrepressible attraction of hope. His near-contemporary, the greatest of all Italian poets, Dante Alighieri (1265-1321), describes a conversation with St. James, known elsewhere as "the apostle of hope," in Canto 25 of the world-famous epic *Paradise*.

"A *bandon hope, all you who enter here*" *is the inscription written above the very portals of Satan's infernal kingdom.*

In the conversation, Dante's guide in heaven tells him that he will be granted special permission to travel from Egypt to Jerusalem because he has shown a special demonstration of hope in his life. "Hope," Dante's character in Paradise says, "is a sure expectation of future glory, which divine grace produces, and preceding merit."[12] More poignantly, however, Dante makes clear that in hell itself the absence of hope is the preeminent characteristic. "Abandon hope, all you who enter here" is the inscription written above the very portals of Satan's infernal kingdom.

ENEMIES OF HOPE—FEAR, DESPAIR, PRESUMPTION

One of the opposites of hope is fear. Roman Catholic theologians in particular have often examined the connection of the two, fear so often being the spur to true hope. "The association of hope and fear is brought out in many passages of Scripture," says the *New Catholic Encyclopedia,* referring among other places to Psalm 39:4 ("Show me, O Lord, my life's end and the number of my days; let me know how fleeting is my life") and Romans 11:20 ("But they [the unbelieving Jews of the Old Testament period] were broken off by unbelief, and you stand by faith. Do not be arrogant, but be afraid"). "Both are necessary," this authoritative source continues. "Hope without fear degenerates into presumption; fear without hope leads to despair."[13]

For Pieper, it is not so much fear as man's awareness of his creaturehood, his fragility before God, that accompanies true hope. He writes: "The uncertainty of human existence cannot be totally removed. But it can be 'overcome'—by hope, and only by hope."[14]

While fear is one of the opposites of hope, so are two other negative and indeed sinful attitudes: despair and presumption. Fear is the negative aspect of the expectation; hope is the positive indicator. If you do not "hope" for a sunny day tomorrow, you are quite likely to "fear" that it will rain. In this sense, fear is the opposite of hope when hope is a near or even an immediate expectation. But fear in another sense is also a sin, an imperfect fear of the Lord. We are commanded to "fear the Lord," but this meaning of the word *fear* in this context is closer to "reverence and respect" than "be terrified of."

In the Letter to the Hebrews, the writer urges us, because we have in Jesus "a great high priest," to "approach the throne of grace with confidence" (Heb 4:15, 16), an attitude that is certainly the opposite of one of terror. Hence, being fearful in our attitude toward God is undeniably a sin. That is why Pieper, commenting on the relationship of faith to fear, notes, "Fear of the Lord and the theological virtue of hope are naturally ordered to one another; they complement one another."[15] The Frankish saint Paschasius Radbert adds, "Holy fear guards the summit of hope."[16]

But a greater and more dangerous opposite quality of hope is despair. "To despair," said St. Isidore (1385-1463), "is to descend into hell."[17] Considering Dante's description of hell and the forbidding words on its portals, he is correct. St. Augustine adds: "There are two things that kill the soul, despair and false hope."[18] Despair was traditionally regarded by the Catholic church as a sin because it threatened man's moral existence.

The traditional view of sloth, arising from the medieval scheme of the seven deadly sins, was that despair actually started with sloth—*acedia* in Latin. Sloth, in this understanding of the word, is not at all straight-forward laziness—say, the unwillingness of a student to study or a worker to do his or her job properly—but a spiritual indolence, a slovenly carelessness about spiritual things.

A careless Christian who says, "I'll get around to it sometime," when admonished to pray more or study the Bible, would be demonstrating this kind of sloth. As Pieper points out, it can quite happily coexist with workaholism: in fact, it often does. He elaborates with his usual cogency:

> As a capital sin, sloth is man's joyless, ill-tempered, and narrow-minded self-seeking rejection of the nobility of the children of God with all the obligations it entails.... Despair (except perhaps, one's awareness of it) is not destroyed by "work," but only by that clear-sighted magnanimity that courageously expects and has confidence in the greatness of its own nature and by the grace-filled impetus of the hope of eternal life.[19]

The third enemy of hope in this classical understanding of the theological virtue by the Roman Catholic church is presumption. This is in some ways as careless as the *acedia* that leads to despair. Presumption takes the view that, salvation and eternal life now being assured the believer, he or she need not humbly rely upon genuine faith and hope to lead one steadily along the pilgrim's road of the walk of faith.

It is, Pieper explains, "an attitude of mind that fails to accept the reality of the futurity and 'arduousness' that characterizes eternal life."[20] Another way of putting it is to say that a person will become so complacent about his or her salvation, positionally accomplished through faith in Jesus Christ, that he or she will veer over into spiritual pride and spiritual laziness. Pieper sums it up in this way:

> One who looks only at the justice of God is as little able to hope as is one who sees only the mercy of God. Both fall prey to hopelessness— one to the hopelessness of despair, the other to the hopelessness of presumption. Only hope is able to comprehend the reality of God that surpasses all antitheses, to know that his mercy is identical with his justice and his justice with his mercy.[21]

"HOPE IS A LITTLE SLIP OF A GIRL…"

Such a view of the opposite of hope serves as a warning that hope the virtue is neither idly acquired nor carelessly practiced. But it would be very wrong to think of hope in terms of stern admonitions against the dangers of its opposites. One of the most striking poems in twentieth-century French literature, for example, is none other than an epic poem on hope by the French poet Charles Péguy. Entitled *Threshold of the Mystery of the Second Virtue,* or *Porche du mystère de la deuxième vertu,* and published in 1911, the poem depicts hope as a delightful child who is a frolicking companion of faith and love. Péguy writes:

> Faith is a loyal Wife.
> Charity [i.e., love] is a Mother.
> A loving mother, all heart.
> Or an elder sister who is like a mother.
> Hope is a little slip of a girl.[22]

As for Faith and Charity, Péguy in his inimitable, charming way describes them as two lonely old ladies whose line would die out if they did not have hope to continue after them. He has them think these thoughts:

They know that they are two generous women.
Two women of promise.
Two women who have something to do in life.
And that through this little girl they are bringing up they hold all
time and eternity itself in the hollow of their hands.[23]

Péguy's God in this poem speaks in the charming, bantering manner of
a kindly old French peasant. Surprisingly, the effect is not at all irreverent
but one that attributes to God a sheer delight in his children, above all
when they hope. Musing aloud, God in Péguy's poem speaks as follows:

But Hope, says God, that astonishes me.
Even me.
...That's astounding and it's easily the greatest wonder of Our grace
And I'm astounded by it myself.
... Hope is a supernatural virtue by which we confidently expect from
God his grace in this world and eternal glory in the next.[24]

Péguy's poem is neither a dilettantish foray into theology using the
vehicle of poetry nor a clever exercise in character portrayal. At the time
he wrote it, he was experiencing a deep crisis in his own life, brought on
largely by the breakdown of affection in his marriage. By his own
admission, working on the *Porche*, a 150-page epic, changed his life.
"People like us always have as much faith and as much charity as we
need," he wrote a friend. "It is hope we may be lacking, and I got it
through writing my *Porche*."[25]

Shortly before his death in 1914 Péguy had more reflections on the
subject:

[Hope] is the source of life, for she is the one who constantly breaks
habits. She is the germ of a spiritual birth. She is the spring and the
giving forth of grace, for she is the one who constantly strips away that
deadly surface of habit.[26]

Robert Royal writes this about the meaning of hope for Péguy:

[Hope is] not simply an idea that you grasp and then go about your
business. It is a living force—perhaps the living cosmic force—that
enables us to gaze at the fullness of reality, in fact brings us into closer

contact with the real.... Hope became, for Péguy, a central occupation, as *amore* had been for Dante.[27]

CROSSING THE THRESHOLD OF HOPE

What was it that Péguy discovered about hope in his work on the poem? Royal believes that one of the most remarkable insights the Frenchman delivered was how hope really originates with God as an act of grace. The word *grace* might from one perspective be defined as the unmerited gift from God of a special spiritual virtue or insight during a time of personal challenge. All theologians have defined the theological virtue of hope as being dependent upon God's grace.

But the uniqueness of Péguy's insight lies in his sense that God had prior hope in us before we ourselves were enabled by his grace to hope. It is a breathtaking concept, and Royal puts it this way:

> We are presented with 1) the unbelievable power of hope, in fact that it is based on God's prior hope in us, but also 2) the realization that the temporal hope and the eternal hope, so to speak, are mutually dependent on one another, and that even God Himself must continue to hope after seeing how His creatures behave every day.[28]
>
> ... Many poets have written of the search for faith or the need for charity, but no poet has written of hope with such sheer mastery.[29]

One far more prominent twentieth-century Roman Catholic thinker, who at least in his youth was a poet, who has thought much about the topic of hope, is Karol Wojtyla, otherwise known as Pope John Paul II. His 1994 best-selling book, a compendium of long responses to written interview questions on a broad range of topics, is appropriately entitled *Crossing the Threshold of Hope*.[30]

The Italian journalist Vittorio Messori, who compiled and edited the questions and their responses from the Pope, goes far to explain the Pope's personality and motivation in his introduction to the book. "This is a Pope," he says, "who is impatient in his apostolic zeal... who—evangelically—wants to shout from the rooftops (today crowded with television antennae) that there is hope."[31] John Paul II himself certainly confirms this judgment in the course of the book.

"What is the Gospel?" he asks rhetorically, early in the book. "It is a grand affirmation of the world and of man, because it is the revelation of the truth about God. God is the primary source of joy and hope for man."[32] He continues:

> Because the Pope is a witness of Christ and a minister of the Good News, he is a man of joy and a man of hope, a man of the fundamental affirmation of the value of existence, the value of creation and hope in the future life. Naturally, this is neither a naïve joy nor a vain hope.[33]

In fact, immediately after his installation as Pope on October 22, 1978, John Paul II went out among the young people in St. Peter's Square in Rome and told them, "You are the hope of the Church and of the world. You are my hope."[34] It was an almost prophetic thing to say for the supreme pontiff of the Roman Catholic church, the man who has expressed the wish to be still alive and strong enough to lead his large portion of global Christendom into the third millennium.

HOPE AMONG PROTESTANTS

The mainstream of the Protestant tradition has also always had exponents of the idea of hope, and few more powerful than John Calvin himself. Contemplating the forbidding challenges that early Reformation thinkers and communities faced from the hostile surrounding world of sixteenth-century Catholicism, Calvin was forthright about hope. He asked, "What would become of us if we did not take our stand on hope, and if your heart did not hasten beyond this world through the midst of the darkness upon the path illumined by the word and the Spirit of God?"[35] For Calvin, hope was a great process of anticipating the things that Christians believed God had promised:

> Thus faith believes God to be true, hope awaits the time when this truth shall be manifested; faith believes that he is our Father, hope anticipates that he will ever show himself to be a Father toward us; faith believes that eternal life has been given to us, hope anticipates that it will some time be revealed; faith is the foundation upon which hope rests, hope nourishes and sustains faith.[36]

Calvin's emphasis on hope was taken up by the central streams of the Protestant tradition. In *The Book of Common Prayer* of the Episcopal church, hope rings out of the pages of time-honored prayers. Some examples:

From the Collect for Tuesday in Easter Week: "Grant that we, who have been raised with him, may abide in his presence and rejoice in the hope of eternal glory."[37]

From Proper 28 (the Sunday closest to November 16): "Blessed Lord, who caused all holy Scriptures to be written for our learning: Grant us so to hear them, read, mark, learn, and inwardly digest them, that we may embrace and ever hold fast the blessed hope of everlasting life, which you have given us in our Savior Jesus Christ; who lives and reigns with you and the Holy Spirit, one God, for ever and ever."[38]

From prayers to be offered in the event of Christian martyrdom: "Grant that we may always be ready to give a reason for the hope that is in us, and to suffer gladly for the sake of our Lord Jesus Christ..."[39]

From the examination of a bishop-elect: "Your heritage is the faith of the patriarchs, prophets, apostles, and martyrs, and those of every generation who have looked to God in hope."[40]

From the Catechism:

Q. What is Christian hope?
A. The Christian hope is to live with confidence in newness and fullness of life, and to await the coming of Christ in glory, and the completion of God's purpose for the world.
Q. What, then, is our assurance as Christians?
A. Our assurance as Christians is that nothing, not even death, shall separate us from the love of God which is in Christ Jesus our Lord.[41]

Meanwhile, Calvin's own interpretation of hope as the principal guide through the thickets of distress and persecution, in which Christians have sometimes found themselves, has flourished intermittently since the sixteenth century. It surfaced with particular vigor after World War II in a school of Protestant theology responding to the damage to Christian faith in Europe that Hitler's bestial leadership of Nazi Germany had wrought.

Many Christian thinkers wanted to know whether the Christian faith provided any unique answer to the universal despair brought on by the war's destruction. They were also curious about the remarkable phenomena of survival in the German and Japanese concentration, prison, and internment camps. Why had some people survived triumphantly, and why had some succumbed so easily? As we shall see in the pages to come, imprisonment has sometimes provided the most fertile ground of all for the Christian hope to take root and blossom.

In the case of the Protestant theologians who sought to develop a "theology of hope" in the late 1940s and early 1950s, the issue of hope was more fundamental than the question of why some prison inmates acquired and deployed it to save their lives while others did not. What the inquiring Christian thinkers of the day needed was a sense that hope was so much part of the Christian view of life that it would be the perfect companion to faith when faith wavered.

The best-known exponent of this new, elevated concept of hope was the German theologian Jurgen Moltmann (b.1926). Not content to see hope as merely a passive ingredient of a faith strong enough to cope with concentration camps, Moltmann wanted to define hope as a yeast that would stir Christians up always to be divinely discontented with the status quo, injustice, and other maladies of any age. He placed hope on perhaps the highest level among the three theological virtues that it could ever reasonably hope for. Faith and hope were essential to each other, he argued, but hope played the initiating role in the relationship:

> Thus in the Christian life, faith has the priority, but hope the primacy. Without faith's knowledge of Christ, hope becomes a utopia and remains hanging in the air. But without hope, faith falls to pieces, becomes a faint-hearted and ultimately a dead faith. It is through faith that man finds the path of true life, but it is only hope that keeps him on that path. Thus it is that faith in Christ gives hopes its assurance. Thus it is that hope gives faith in Christ its breath and leads it into life.[42]

This concept is very similar to Péguy's view that hope is what conducts people boldly into a sense of the real, because only with hope can people cope with the suffering and disappointments of life. "Hope goes on its way through the midst of happiness and pain," Moltmann explains, "because in the promises of God it can see a future for the transient, the dying and the dead. That is why it can be said that living without hope is like no longer living. Hell is hopelessness."[43]

But at the same time that hope offers comfort and assurance in life's valleys, Moltmann insists, it makes people restless for God's kingdom and his justice:

Hope constantly provokes and produces thinking of an anticipatory kind in love to man and the world, in order to give shape to the newly dawning possibilities in the light of the promised future... Always the Christian hope has had a revolutionary effect in this sense on the intellectual history of the society affected by it.[44]

For a contemporary of Moltmann, the Swiss Protestant thinker Emil Brunner, it is the Christian hope in this fermenting sense that is the answer to the totally secular and—by Brunner's reckoning—totally false idea of human progress that has been proposed by secular thinkers since the Enlightenment. Brunner argues that the whole idea of progress was "a rationalization and secularization of the Christian hope. It was by Christianity that mankind was taught to hope," he adds, "that is, to look to the future for the realization of the true meaning of life."[45]

Yet this secularized view of life, Brunner asserts, a notion of progress given a cosmic dimension by the dogmatic enthronement upon Western intellectual thought of nineteenth-century Darwinism, has been destroyed by the horrors of modern warfare epitomized by the explosion of the first atomic bomb at Hiroshima. Of course, in Brunner's day, Hiroshima was an easily recognizable metaphor for war in general.

HOPE AND OPTIMISM

A major insight of Brunner into the issue of Christian hope is to distinguish hope from optimism. "Christians... are not optimists," he explains. "There is no optimism in the New Testament; optimism is a mark of the eighteenth and nineteenth centuries" (in other words, of the false view that science had enabled the quality of life to become better and better).[46]

Other Protestant thinkers have come to impressively similar conclusions about optimism. Writing in the chapter on Hope in their book *The Art of Living*, Dietrich and Alice Von Hildebrand, German writers active in the 1950s and 1960s, make this point:

Because of the misleading looseness of our use of words, we are often tempted to say that an optimistic person is full of hope, that he is never cast down, that he keeps looking forward to a carefree and enjoyable future. But this attitude has nothing to do with hope; for in optimism we are facing a purely dispositional trait, a purely immanent tendency which is totally deprived of the character of a response.[47]

The Von Hildebrands focus tightly on optimism as a trait of temperament no different in essence from other naturally inherited or environmentally formed traits. Though they do not explicitly make the point that a person's actions might quite incidentally be virtuous or vicious according to the possession of, say, a reserved personality or a violent temper, they clearly view optimism in this light. It has nothing to do with hope, they stress, for two reasons. First, optimism is unconnected to objective reality. Second, it is not in itself a conscious response to a situation. The authors explain:

> Optimism is essentially a sort of inner dynamism, a propelling force which keeps one going; but it is simultaneously coupled with a sort of blindness, for the optimistic person does not see the objective character of a situation, and then respond with optimism, but he is optimistic on principle, and this very disposition precisely blinds him to the objective character of the situation.... Optimism can be compared to a fuel, and the very moment a person runs out of this fuel, his optimism comes to a sudden and unforeseen halt.[48]

For Brunner, optimism's weakness in facing reality has led to a profound misunderstanding of human life itself by secular intellectuals since the time of the eighteenth-century Enlightenment. Since World War II in particular, he nevertheless says forcefully, and specifically since the atomic bomb was dropped on Japan at Hiroshima, "the world does not believe in progress any more.... It has become evident that the basic error of the idea of universal progress lies in the fact that progress in knowledge is not accompanied by a corresponding progress of moral forces."[49]

Brunner observes that the absence of actual land warfare on American soil during the two world wars of this century has enabled "the ghost of progressivist optimism" to continue hovering around intellectual circles in the country. At the same time, he warns that this mood will not last indefinitely. "But it is only a question of years," he warns, "—of a few years I should say—when this religion of progress will die out even in America. But if this hope of two centuries goes, what hope will then remain?"[50]

TRUE HOPE FOR THE CHRISTIAN

What indeed? For Brunner there is only one plausible idea of progress for which one can honestly hope, and that is the expression of hope for the growth of the Kingdom of God within history. "The hope of the Christian," he says,

> is for the future perfection of God's Kingdom in the reign of glory, in eternal life, and in the eternal Kingdom. The hope of the Christian, therefore, is both personal and universal.... A Christian cannot lead a merely private life; he is committed to the work of God in the world; he takes part in God's world plan. He is not concerned primarily about his own personal salvation; he is concerned with God's concern, which is for the world.[51]

This concern for the world is echoed by prominent Christians who have thought long and hard about the impact of the gospel on global culture. One of them is the distinguished Bible scholar and Christian commentator Carl F. Henry:

> Hope for the Christian is not divorced from faith and reason, or from history. The forfeiture of hope is often the last blow before a person loses mental stability. In larger social context a pervasive melancholy often presages the breakdown of a culture. Christianity offers a living hope, and sufficient reason for it. It carries assurance that God is at once Lord of the future and Sovereign of the present. That is all the reason one needs for confronting the very crumbling expectations of modernity with the enduring principles of Christianity.[52]

Billy Graham, who has perhaps had more direct dealings with political leaders from countless countries around the world than any comparable evangelist in history, agrees that "with so much chaos all around us, there is need for hope in the world." For Graham, that hope extends not simply to what can be accomplished in the foreseeable future through possession of the Christian virtues, but to the return of Jesus Christ himself. When that happens, Graham says, there will indeed be "a glorious new social order."[53]

Emil Brunner himself ties together in his concluding comments both this concept of hope encouraging the Christian to set his sights on nothing less than the return of Christ, and the deeply personal, faith-linked promise of hope in individual lives. He writes:

> Therefore the promise in Christ, the goal that is opened to us by faith as the content of hope is world redemption, world salvation. Eternal life is merely the personal aspect of this great hope, the greatest possible hope. This knowledge about the future is based on a fact, the fact of which we have spoken before. For those who do not believe in this fact, all that we have said about hope may be a great illusion. But for those who do believe in that fact, it is the good news of hope.[54]

For the Von Hildebrands the most important facet of hope is its inevitable foundation on the reality of God. As they put it: "Every act of hoping is grounded in God."[55] This, they say, has gigantic consequences in human behavior. "Authentic hope," they argue, is "a radical non-acceptance of evil as being final, as being the last word." The non-acceptance, though, is not a defiant, angry shaking of the fist at reality, an impotent revolt against reality. "In revolt," they explain,

> rejection is impotent. I knock my head against the wall. Whereas in hope, while seeing that humanly speaking, a situation is doomed, I refuse to "close" time. I refuse to "petrify" a situation, to "freeze" it in its tragedy. In hope, I always transcend the framework of earthly finitude. I liberate myself from the phenomenon of "it is all over" and trust that this darkness will be changed into light, that this death is a passage toward resurrection. In fact, hope is a response to God as a loving Creator; in hope I trust the creative power of God "who can make all things new."[56]

Hope for the Hildebrands is thus always "hope in," meaning a trust in God's perennial and unshakable goodness. In this sense it works truly hand in hand with faith, not simply as a theological virtue that points men and women toward God but as a weapon in true spiritual warfare. This is not blind hope, not the gambler's last, desperate throw of the cosmic dice, but a confident demonstration of trust in God's power and love—the same trust the Apostle Peter first demonstrated when he stepped over the wave-lapped side of his fishing boat to walk on water at his master's command.

True Christian hope is thus inevitably an aspect of true spiritual praise, a component of the Christian's humble, repentant, yet ultimately bold response to what Jesus Christ accomplished on the cross. Author and speaker Leanne Payne, whose Pastoral Care Ministries have transformed thousands of lives by allowing the power of the cross, especially accompanied by praise, to transform individuals inwardly, frankly describes hope in this context as one among a number of spiritual weapons:

> These weapons are intimately allied to repentance (that state of godly sorrow which ends in salvation and the knowledge of holiness), faith (trust in God Who is with us and in His power), hope (we are transients, pilgrims headed for a city whose architect and builder is God), and love…. The power to repent, believe, hope and love, indeed, all of the great Christian virtues leap into life and operation when we truly preach the Word of the Cross, lifting it high.[57]

Does this suggest, as some people might imagine, that hope is a sort of theological smile button that is donned at the beginning of each day and which therefore somehow magically wards off setbacks, hurts, and even tragedy? Nothing could be further from the truth. As all writers on hope have either explicitly or implicitly conveyed, hope is authentic precisely because it is first cousin to suffering.

As we saw in chapter 7, Paul quite explicitly makes this point in Romans 5:2-5: "But we also rejoice in our sufferings, because we know that suffering produces perseverance; perseverance, character; and character, hope. And hope does not disappoint us, because God has poured out his love into our hearts by the Holy Spirit, whom he has given us."

"HOPE DOES DISAPPOINT US"

"Hope does not disappoint us." How totally true, the more so because it was said by one who suffered so grievously in his own ministry. A modern writer who has thought a lot on this subject is Eugene Petersen, author of a highly acclaimed, modern-day translation of the New Testament.[58]

Petersen notes that Christians who experience suffering of any kind are often surrounded by people wanting to counsel them and then inundated with advice on how to cope with the grim experience they are traversing.

"But none of that is what we need," he says. "We need hope. We need to know that we are in relation to God. We need to know that suffering is part of what it means to be human and not something alien."

Petersen explains that "hoping is not dreaming. It is not spinning an illusion of fantasy," he says, "to protect us from our boredom or our pain. It means a confident alert expectation that God will do what he said he will do."[59]

And this raises an interesting question: Just what has God said that he will do? It has often been said, not entirely as a wisecrack, "Those who don't expect anything from God won't be disappointed." On the other hand, those who expect much will certainly not be disappointed, either.

One of the greatest of all English missionaries was William Carey (1761-1834), who set forth for India in June 1793, the same year in which the grotesque Festival of Reason was brought into France's Notre Dame Cathedral, the year in which the horrors of the Terror during the French Revolution took place, and the year William Kant's "beheading" of belief in God occurred, according to the German poet Heine.

A*ttempt great things for God.*
 Expect great things from God.

Carey became famous for a saying that has inspired generations of missionaries since then: "Attempt great things for God. Expect great things from God." His own "attempts" were gargantuan: six entire translations of the Bible and twenty-three translations of the New Testament into Indian languages before he died in 1834. Yet for the first five and a half years, Carey had not a single convert. Was he discouraged? At times, probably. Were his expectations of God unfounded? Hardly.

Though Carey obviously did not live to see the gigantic evangelistic harvest from his own efforts, we can see today how far his expectations of God were borne out. According to the authoritative *World Christian Encyclopedia*, there were a total of 27 million Christians in India in 1980, and at the rate of growth of believers, the number was likely to grow to 49 million by the year 2,000.[60] Carey's theology was sound. He had inherited it from a source we don't always associate with hope, even though they arguably had more of it than any other generation of Christians in the history of the planet. They were, of course, the Puritans.

TEN

The Puritans:
Hope and History

A s many Christian pilgrims have discovered, coming across the writings of the Puritans after exploring the rich forest of Christian writings of all ages and cultures is like suddenly stumbling upon a stand of tall, stately trees that tower over every growing thing around them. Indeed, the outstanding British expert on Puritan Christianity, J.I. Packer, has forthrightly compared the spiritual depth, godliness, and sheer insight of the English Puritans to California's giant redwoods, towering more than three hundred feet high from a narrow strip of California coastline.

"As redwoods attract the eye, because they overtop other trees," Packer writes in his brilliant account of Puritan spirituality,

> so the mature holiness and seasoned fortitude of the great Puritans shine before us as a kind of beacon light, overtopping the stature of the majority of Christians in most eras, and certainly so in this age of crushing urban collectivism, when Western Christians sometimes feel and often look like ants in an anthill and puppets on a string.[1]

WHO WERE THE PURITANS?

The Puritans were primarily English Protestant Christians, both clergy and laypeople, of the period approximately 1560-1700. They sought to purify public worship in English churches at a time when priests in the Church of England were frequently ignorant and morally backslidden and when English Protestantism was running out of spiritual steam.

English Puritanism had a major influence on the Christianity of the early New England settlements, especially in the 1630s and 1640s, when the New Englanders sided overwhelmingly with the English Parliament in the years leading up to and during the English Civil War of 1642-1649. Thus, in one sense, English Puritanism as a visible phenomenon in England all but disappeared after the restoration of King Charles II to the English throne in 1660. His restoration put an end to the experiment of England as a republic.

Yet the impact of Puritan godliness, however much ridiculed in the decadent era of Charles II—the so-called "Merry Monarch"—was felt for nearly three centuries in many areas of English national life. Overseas, English military discipline and national vigor during the Cromwellian period, 1649-1658, made England the most respected and feared nation in Europe.

A dozen decades of nineteenth-century worldliness and twentieth-century skepticism have succeeded in transforming the popular image of the Puritans from family-oriented, devout, generous, and God-fearing folk into stern, superstition-prone, tyrannical theocrats all but determined to stamp out fun whenever it reared its unpleasant head. Among serious scholars of the period, it is fair to say, this caricature-like understanding of the Puritans has been replaced for at least fifty years on both sides of the Atlantic by a growing admiration of the astonishing achievement of the Puritans, above all in learning.

Even a severe critic of Christian fundamentalist anti-intellectualism like Richard Hofstadter, in his classic study of the role of this phenomenon on American history, is deeply respectful of the Puritans. "It is doubtful that any community ever had more faith in the value of learning and intellect than Massachusetts Bay," he writes. "Having established a learned and literary class, the Puritan community gave this class great scope for the realization of their gifts."[2]

Yet the hostile image of the Puritans dies hard in the popular American and British imagination, particularly in an era when standards of personal morality are obviously in decline even among many professing Christians. It is important, therefore, to grasp just how revolutionary and influential the Puritans were in the depth of their biblical exegesis, the honesty of their spiritual self-examination, and the brilliance of their insight into human behavior.

The introduction to a popular 1960s edition of John Bunyan's *Pilgrim's Progress* acknowledges this. "Puritanism has been misconceived as restrictive moral prohibitions, weighted down by sexual guilt," the writer of the introduction observed, but corrected it by adding, "In the mid-seventeenth century it was a fiery religious and social dynamic resembling contemporary [1960s-era] Marxism more than modern Funda-mentalism."[3]

It may surprise some people today to learn that more than any other generation of Christians, the Puritans probably came closest to a mature understanding of the true benefits—and costs—of religious liberty and of the subtle difficulties Christians always face when allying evangelical zeal too closely to the levers of state power. "They were great souls serving a great God," Packer sums them up. "Visionary and practical, idealist and realistic too, goal-oriented and methodical, they were great believers, great hopers, great doers, and great sufferers."[4]

Above all, the Puritans were great "hopers." Iain Murray, a pioneering scholar of the role that the concept of hope played in Puritan theology, missiology, and spirituality, puts it this way:

> There was an attitude toward history and to the world which distinguished them as men of hope. In their own day, this hope came to expression in pulpits and in books, in Parliament and upon battlefields, but it did not end there. The outlook they had done so much to inspire went on for nearly two hundred years after their own age and its results were manifold. It colored the spiritual thought of the American colonies; it taught men to expect great outpourings of the Holy Spirit; it prepared the way to the new age of world-missions; and it contributed largely to that sense of destiny which came to characterize the English-speaking Protestant nations.[5]

That, of course, is truly a stupendous achievement. In fact, if even half of Murray's assessment holds true, then it suggests that the Puritans have more to teach Christians today about hope than most of the rest of Christian history put together. Even a cursory look at the enormous output of the great Puritan writers, almost all of it truly meaty, confirms this impression.

PURITANS AND THE HOPE OF HEAVEN

One of the best starting points for an illustration of the Puritan view of hope is found in what is by far the outstanding novel of the sixteenth century, and one of the most enduring Christian novels of all time, *Pilgrim's Progress* by John Bunyan (1628-1688). Translated into innumerable languages, and having that unique quality of a literary classic, which transcends cultures and epochs in its universal human appeal, Bunyan's masterpiece is nevertheless an orthodox Christian work of immense spiritual depth. It is, of course, an allegory of the spiritual life for an ordinary but devout, and indeed "converted" (born-again), Christian. It is also an allegory for a journey, a spiritual journey.

O ne notable strength of the Puritans, setting them far apart from Western Christians today, was the firmness of their grip on the biblical teaching about the hope of heaven.

Just as Thomas Aquinas and medieval Roman Catholic Christendom viewed the Christian life as a journey and the Christian as a wayfarer or traveler, so the Puritans (while disagreeing strongly with much Roman Catholic doctrine and practice) focused on the Christian life as a journey toward heaven. Comments J.I. Packer:

> One notable strength of the Puritans, setting them far apart from Western Christians today, was the firmness of their grip on the biblical teaching about the hope of heaven. Basic to their pastoral care was their understanding of the Christian's present life as a journey home, and they made much of encouraging God's people to look ahead and feast their hearts on what is to come.[6]

At different times in *Pilgrim's Progress*, the principal character, Christian, is accompanied by two other pilgrims. One is Faithful, who is martyred at Vanity Fair. Another is Hopeful, who becomes Christian's companion after Faithful's death. One of the most frightening episodes for Christian is being imprisoned by the Giant of Despair in the dungeon of the Giant's castle, along with Hopeful. The incident reflects Bunyan's own struggles with what today we would call depression during his spiritual walk.

Despite beatings by both Giant and his wife, wonderfully named Diffidence, neither Hopeful nor Christian is entirely intimidated. This causes the two ogres to speculate in a homey fashion just before going to bed why they have not yet succeeded in completely breaking their two prisoners.

"I fear," Diffidence suggests, "that they live in hope that some will come to relieve them, or that they have pick-locks about them; by the means of which they hope to escape."

"And sayest though so, my dear," the Giant responds cozily, "I will therefore search them in the morning."[7]

But the morning proves to be too late. After praying from midnight until morning, Christian remembers that he has a key on his person called "promise," that he believes will open the doors out of the castle of Despair. Sure enough, the key works on all the various doors and gates, and the two pilgrims make good their escape.

The insight was a very important and a very familiar one for Bunyan's Puritan readers (and many non-Puritans since then). With the conviction that the Bible was the final authority and source of God's love, mercy, and provision to his people, the Puritans always looked to it for divine assurance in times of uncertainty.

William Gurnall (1616-1679) was a Puritan whose book *The Christian in Complete Armour* has had incalculable influence on outstanding Christians since the seventeenth century. These have included such notable men as John Newton, the ex-slave trader and composer of "Amazing Grace," and the nineteenth-century evangelist Charles Spurgeon. Gurnall connected hope directly to God's promises. He wrote:

The hope of salvation supports the believer in the greatest afflictions. The Christian's patience is his back, where he carries his burdens; and some afflictions are so heavy that he needs a broad one to carry them. But if hope does not lay the pillow of the promise between his back and his burden, the least cross will prove too much. Therefore this promise is called "the patience of hope in our Lord Jesus Christ" (1 Thes 1:3).[8]

Gurnall's understanding of promises and hope was not limited to consolations of the individual in times of distress. It formed the entire worldview of the Puritan era. The Puritans faced such immense opposition to their desire to base Christian freedom and Christian authority solely on the Bible that they fought a civil war in England to gain it. And they looked with hope to the eventual evangelization of the world.

George Newton (1602-1681), who was a pastor at Taunton, in Somerset, drew a powerful doctrine of missionary hope from Christ's last prayer to his Father in the presence of his disciples in John 17:26: "I have made you known to them, and will continue to make you known in order that the love you have for me may be in them and that I myself may be in them." Newton concluded:

Let our hearts be full of hope in reference to this business.... Our Savior's words are a promise to the Father, what he will do in after times for his people: saith he, "I will declare thy name" to them. And therefore as it is our duty to believe the promise, so to expect the good things promised. To be continually in a waiting frame, looking and hearkening after the accomplishment of this excellent work of his, spying if we can see the daybreak, and the Father's name shine forth to other nations who never had a glimpse of it by any gospel revelation, till in the end, "from the rising of the sun unto the going down of the same, his name be great among the Gentiles," according to that prophecy relating to these latter times and ages of the world (Mal 1:11).[9]

HOPE IN BIBLICAL PROPHECY

A conviction of future global evangelization was not based solely, in the Puritans' minds, on the promises of Jesus. The immensely hope-filled attitude toward missionary outreach was based on an intense study of biblical prophecy in the Old Testament and Pauline prophecy in the New Testament about God's blessings reaching all of the Gentiles. The famous New England divine John Eliot (1604-1690) crossed the Atlantic in 1631 to minister to the English settlers in Massachusetts. Later, at the age of forty, he started out to learn the Algonquin Indian language to communicate the gospel to them.

In 1649, with the Puritans now victorious in the English Civil War, Parliament itself established the Society for the Propagation of the Gospel in New England. A year earlier, twelve prominent English Puritans addressed both Lords and Commons of the English Parliament in their preface to a work describing Puritan missionary efforts in New England. "The utmost ends of the earth are designed and promised to be in time the possessions of Christ," they wrote:

This little we see is something in hand, to earnest to us those things which are in hope; something in possession, to assure us of the rest in promise, when the ends of the earth shall see his glory, and the kings of the world shall become the kingdoms of the Lord and his Christ, when he shall have dominion from sea to sea, and they that dwell in the wilderness shall bow before him.[10]

Like everything else in the Bible, the Puritans took biblical prophecy literally. Their reading of Scripture convinced them of two things that formed the foundation of their hope for the Christian future.

The first was that Christ would not return until the knowledge of the Lord had indeed filled the whole earth, until world evangelization was complete.

The second was that the Jews would turn to Jesus as their Messiah en masse before the Messiah came back to Jerusalem.

Since neither of these occurrences had yet transpired, it behooved Christians, the Puritans were convinced, to work with encouragement toward these goals. "Let no man despair," said Richard Sibbes, preaching at Cambridge until his death in 1635, "nor, as I said before, let us despair of the conversion of those that are savages in other parts. How bad soever they be, they are of the world, and if the gospel be preached to them, Christ will be 'believed on in the world.'"[11]

Sibbes, like most of the Puritans, connected the future worldwide Christian awakening to the turning of the Jews to Jesus. "And when the fullness of the Gentiles is come in, then comes the conversion of the Jews. Why may we not expect it? These were the peoples of God."[12]

The word *conversion*, of course, has an unpleasant ring today to many Jews because it smacks of persecution of them in the past—and not so distant past, either—in supposedly "Christian" communities, and of coercion against them to cease being Jews and become Christians. But in Puritan times the understanding of conversion of the Jews was not that the Jews should become Gentiles, but that they should, as Jews, believe that Jesus was indeed their own long-awaited Messiah.

This form of conversion, a change of heart rather than a change of national or ethnic or even religious identity, was to be accomplished solely through spiritual means. This is made clear again and again by Puritan writers. Thomas Goodwin wrote that Christians ought to accept that some of their prayers would simply not be answered in their lifetimes, including "the calling of the Jew, the utter downfall of God's enemies, the flourishing of the gospel."[13]

So positive was the attitude of many Puritans toward the Jews that none other than Oliver Cromwell (1599-1658), the Lord Protector of England after the Parliamentary victory in the English Civil War, was convinced that the cause of the gospel in general was connected directly to kindness toward the Jews. In December 1655, he convened a conference in Whitehall to discuss the readmission of the Jews to England, from which they had been driven out nearly three centuries earlier by the English King Edward III (1327-1377).

"GLORY IN HOPE ..."

Cromwell was a devout Puritan who had been converted at the age of twenty-eight, firmly believing the prophetic Scriptures about both global evangelization and the Jewish recognition of the Messiah. He argued forcefully for the Jewish readmission, basing his arguments squarely on Scripture. "Since there is a promise in Holy Scripture of the conversion of the Jews," he said, "I do not know, but the preaching of the Christian religion as it is now in England, without idolatry or superstition, may not conduce to it."[14]

The majority of the conference opposed his specific proposal to permit free entry of Jews to England, but Cromwell secured the personal right to grant individual Jews residence permission. This marks the beginning of a fundamental turning away from the original policy of banning Jews.

Cromwell, not surprisingly, was a man whose personal convictions were filled with biblical hope, even though by temperament he would sometimes succumb to bouts of melancholia. He told Parliament that he would never have played a role in the struggle of Parliament with King Charles unless he had been convinced that God was in the cause. He explained: "If it be of man, I would I had never touched it with a finger. If I had not had a hope fixed in me that this cause and this business was of God, I would many years ago have run from it."[15]

He told Parliament on another occasion that the cause of Parliament could only effectively be carried on by "men in a Christian state: who have works with faith; who know how to lay hold on Christ for remission of sins, till a man be brought to *glory in hope*. Such a hope kindled in men's spirit will actuate them to such ends as you are tending to" [italics in original].[16]

Cromwell's hope, like that of all the Puritans, also extended vigorously to world missions. He wanted to divide the world into four great missions fields and have an English council of missions established that would, essentially, begin strategic planning for evangelization of the entire world. In these aspirations, he was in the mainstream of Puritan spirituality.

His personal chaplain, John Howe (1630-1705), a very young man when he first became associated with Cromwell, was even more convinced that the greatest manifestations of God's grace and involvement in the human condition were still ahead. The conviction—as opposed to mere feeling or "sense"—was important. It suffused the Puritan attitude with hope even at times when the political and spiritual circumstances of England looked bleak. For Howe, as for Gurnall, Goodwin, and all of the others, it was the God-given virtue of hope that kept people's heads above water and provided the ultimate antidote for discouragement. "Plain it is," wrote Howe,

> there is not a more stupefying, benumbing thing in all the world than mere despair. To look upon such a sad face and aspect of things through the world as we have before our eyes; to look upon it despairingly and with apprehension that it never will, never can be better; nothing can more stupefy and bind up the powers of our souls and sink us into a desponding meanness of spirit. But hope is a kind of anticipated enjoyment and gives a present participation in the expected pleasantness of those days, how long soever they may yet be off from us. By such a lively hope we have a presentation, a feeling in our own spirits of what is to come, that should even make our hearts rejoice and our bones to flourish as a herb.[17]

Hope never existed by itself for the Puritans. It was always linked in some way to faith. "If thou hast faith, thou hast Hope," wrote Thomas Preston (1593-1633):

And this distinguisheth a Christian's faith from the faith of reprobates, from the faith of devils, from the temporary faith that others are capable of: you know the devils believe and tremble: He said not, "The devils believe and hope," for they do not. Hope is a property of faith, and where there is faith, there is hope.[18]

Hope, added Preston, "is a lively hope, a hope that sets a man a-work, a hope that purgeth him. For, you know, that which a man hopes for, he will endeavor to bring it to pass, it is such a hope as not to fail you, but will continue as well as faith itself."[19]

For Thomas Watson, faith was "the master-wheel; it sets all the other graces running."[20]

For William Gurnall, hope and faith were "inevitably kin." He added:

Faith and hope are two graces which Christ uses above all others to fill the soul with joy, because these fetch all their wine of joy out of doors. Faith tells the soul what Christ has done and hope revives the soul with news of what he will do.[21]

Gurnall, in fact, wrote at such length and with such eloquence about hope—"the helmet of salvation"—in his *Complete Armour* that we will cite several excerpts at the end of the chapter. It is hard to find any Christian writer, of any epoch or language, who has sculpted for our imagination so exquisitely the role that hope plays in our spiritual lives.

HOPE IN THE SECOND COMING OF CHRIST

But what of the end of the Puritan era? What happened to the magnificent Puritan concept of hope?

The sad answer is that it at first went into eclipse for a season as a motivating element of the Christian life, at least within English Christianity. Later, it was swept pitilessly aside in the nineteenth-century speculation about the timing of the Second Coming of Christ. The eclipse occurred largely because of the exhaustion of the Puritan impulse in the gargantuan struggles of the English Civil War and, after the restoration of Charles II in 1660, both the resurgence of libertine lifestyles at the English court and the enforcement of the Anglican Prayer Book in English churches.

It was not until the evangelical awakening in England in the 1730s and the Great Awakening in America in the same decade that the great Puritan themes of God's sovereign interest in evangelism were sounded again. This time, the name forever associated with the renewal of the idea of hope was Jonathan Edwards (1703-1758).

An academically brilliant youth, Edwards had mastered Latin, Greek, and Hebrew by age thirteen and graduated head of his class at the Collegiate School of Connecticut (later to be Yale University) at the age of seventeen. But it was not until he was twenty-four that he experienced a personal conversion to Christ and embarked on a path of dynamic preaching that affected congregations wherever he went.

Edwards was a staunch Calvinist, a strong believer in God's total sovereignty, and was directly in the Puritan tradition of belief that the Lord himself would foster the work of evangelism through every age and in every country. "From the fall of man, to our day, the work of redemption in its effect has been mainly carried on by remarkable communications of the spirit of God," he wrote.[22]

Edwards was convinced that nothing had occurred to change God's willingness to bring spiritual revival to his people indefinitely throughout history. He acknowledged that men and women might remain "ignorant of the times and seasons which the Father hath put in his power,"[23] but he was as full of conviction as Oliver Cromwell or Richard Sibbes that there would be no insuperable obstacle to the progressive revelation of Christ throughout the world.

This forward-looking, profoundly hope-filled perspective in the Christian future also led him to a conception of the universal church that, for its day, was revolutionary. "It may be hoped," he wrote, "that then [after the gospel has spread extensively on an international scale] many of the Negroes and Indians will be divines, and that excellent books will be published in Africa, in Ethiopia, in Tartary."[24]

As an American, he would have applauded a twentieth-century U.S. president who drew attention to the achievements of an African-American preacher before a national audience in a State of the Union address.[25] He would have rejoiced that the Christian church in China would be one of the fastest-growing communities of Christian believers anywhere in the world.[26]

In England, the conversion of John Wesley (1703-1791) in 1738 and his subsequent joining together with George Whitefield led to what became known as the Evangelical Revival. Though the intense excitement of the early years eventually quieted down, just as the Great Awakening in New England had run out of steam by the mid-1740s, the long-term impact of the revivals was enormous.

In the 1790s, the decade in which William Carey set out for India, several English missionary societies were formed. In addition, John Wesley himself became increasingly concerned about prison reform and the abolition of the slave trade. Just before he died, he wrote a letter to William Wilberforce (1759-1833), then a young member of Parliament, urging him to continue in Wilberforce's campaign to abolish slavery in England. (This was eventually achieved in 1807 in England itself and by 1833 throughout the British empire.)

The Anglican Evangelicals who emerged from the eighteenth-century revivals, and to which Wilberforce belonged, were known as the Clapham Sect. What is striking is that they believed the whole world would eventually be won for Christ and that immense changes for good could occur in English society if convinced Christians quietly went to work within existing institutions. They were filled with hope that the same Holy Spirit who had transformed the life of England in the Puritan era, as well as in the revivals of a century later, was still operating as powerfully as ever throughout the world.

This same conviction was shared by Charles H. Spurgeon, the great nineteenth-century British evangelist who has sometimes been called "the last of the Puritans." Spurgeon's preaching had a powerful impact on the London working classes. He shared the same views on the certainty of an eventual large-scale turning to Jesus Christ on the part of the Jewish people, and of an immense global Christian harvest, that the Puritan preachers had held. "I expect the same power which turned the world upside down once will still continue to do it," he said in a sermon entitled "The Triumph of Christianity."[27]

DARBY AND THE BRETHREN

Yet by Spurgeon's time, a profound change in outlook had come upon much of evangelical Christianity in both England and the U.S. as a result of the interpretation of biblical prophecy by two influential Englishmen, Edward Irving (1792-1834) and J.N. Darby (1800-1882).

Irving, an emotional and compelling speaker, was convinced that the Bible foretold a terrible future judgment of the church, to be followed by the premillennial return of Christ. He attracted a huge following for a while, though his founding of the "Catholic Apostolic Church" in 1830 led to a formal break between him and the London Presbytery of the Church of Scotland. When Irving died of exhaustion at a relatively young age, his role as leader of a new school of Christian prophecy-obsessed believers was taken over by Darby, founder of a highly disciplined evangelical Christian movement called the Brethren.

Darby's role in influencing evangelical thought about biblical prophecy was nothing less than revolutionary. He elaborated a doctrine that had been extremely rare in the previous eighteen centuries of the Christian church, that Christ's appearing before the establishment of his millennial kingdom would be in two stages, the first to be characterized by a secret "rapture" that would remove the church. The second stage would follow the "Great Tribulation," when Jesus would establish his rule on the earth.

These beliefs were generally known as "dispensational" premillennialism, or sometimes simply "dispensationalism," because Darby believed in different "dispensations," or periods of church history. Dispensationalism acquired something of the character of evangelical orthodox doctrine through the influence on the American evangelical scholar C.I. Scofield. The *Scofield Reference Bible*, first published in 1909, became for many evangelical Christians an almost infallible interpretation of the last days before the return of Christ.

This is not the place to examine in detail the various doctrines relating to the return, or second advent, of Jesus Christ. Nor need we take sides in the ongoing debates between millennialism, premillennialism, postmillennialism, and so forth. Two important points need to be made, though. The first is that the Darby interpretation, with the idea of the secret rapture of the saints, was all but unheard of in the entire history of the Christian church until about 1830. The second is that Darby's interpretation of the future of the church in the world introduced right down to our own day a profound pessimism about the long-term value of Christian social action in the manner of Wilberforce, or of the overall prospects of global evangelization.

As for any possibility that the Jews might turn to Jesus as Messiah in large numbers, this idea was completely abandoned. Darby also specifically denied the traditional belief of both Roman Catholics and the Protestant reformers that the church consisted of the "mystical body" of Christian believers worldwide. This, he held, was "unscriptural."[28]

In place of the inspiring Puritan vision that the world would eventually be filled with the knowledge of the Lord as a result of God's supernatural grace and the prayers of the saints of many generations, Darby argued that the only thing really worth hoping for was the quickest possible return of Christ, the rapture of the saints before the Great Tribulation, and the establishment of the millennial kingdom on earth. In an address in Geneva in 1840, Darby made his profound pessimism explicit:

What we are about to consider will tend to shew that, instead of permitting ourselves to hope for a continued progress of good, we must expect a progress of evil; and that the hope of the earth being filled with the knowledge of the Lord before the exercise of His judgment, and the consummation of this judgment on the earth, is delusive.[29]

It is interesting that Darby's views on the end times have been adopted by both Pentecostal/charismatic and Bible Church/fundamentalist wings of American evangelicalism. This is curious, because dispensationalist theologians in the fundamentalist wing tend to believe that the charismatic gifts of the Holy Spirit (tongues, interpretation, prophecy, miracles, etc., in 1 Corinthians 12 and 14) were removed from the church at the end of the apostolic age, at around the end of the first century A.D. This often leads to the view among fundamentalists that any present-day manifestations of the charismatic gifts of the Spirit are counterfeit phenomena. Yet the same view of the Rapture is held by both the fundamentalists and the Pentecostals.

STARTING WITH HOPE AND ENDING WITH HOPE

Individual Christians, of course, must draw their own conclusions as to what the Bible really says about the sequence of events that will precede, in whatever duration of time, the wonderful return of Jesus Christ, with his saints, to rule the world. Certainly, many great missionary works have been accomplished around the world in this century by those who have held premillenialist interpretations of biblical prophecy. Fortunately, a life lived in the power of the Holy Spirit does not depend on this or that view of biblical end times.

Yet it needs to be asked whether the very obvious alienation of the modern secular world from evangelical Christendom, especially in the U.S., does not owe something to the pessimism about the future of the world that is so often conveyed—sometimes with an irritating smugness— by ardent evangelical Christians. Is gloom and doom on a global scale all that Christians really have to offer the world? Or is the case that can be made for the Christian hope—which, as we have seen, isn't at all the same thing as optimism—as valid today for the world as it was in the chaotic seventeenth century, or the gin-soaked London of the eighteenth century, before the Evangelical Revival significantly changed the way ordinary people behaved?

Is gloom and doom on a global scale all that Christians really have to offer the world?

Why should the Lord be any more finished with the world in, say, the year 2,000 than he was in 1650? Or 1350, one of the most calamitous centuries in European history (with the Black Death killing one-third of the population of Europe)? Or 450, when orderly life was being replaced in the Roman Empire by disease, political breakdown, social anarchy, and invasions by waves of barbarous tribes from northern Europe?

In short, to pin the authenticity of the gospel message to the human race on the inevitability of imminent global catastrophe is neither historically sound nor theologically wise. It certainly isn't conducive to an understanding of Christian hope—the glorious assurance of the anchoring of our destiny, both in this life and the next, to the extraordinary act of mercy and love performed on behalf of the human race by God through his Son Jesus Christ.

Consider more of Gurnall's eloquent observations about hope:

Hope brings down such consolation that the afflicted soul can smile even when tears run down the face. This is called "the rejoicing of the hope" (Heb 3:6). And hope never produces more joy than in affliction.

While troubles attack with oppression, the gracious promises anoint with blessings. Hope breaks the alabaster box of the promises over the Christian's head and sends consolations abroad in the soul. And like a precious ointment these comforts exhilarate and refresh the spirit, heal the wounds, and remove the pain.[30]

Hope is the handkerchief that God gently uses to wipe away the tears from the eyes of His people. "Refrain thy voice from weeping, and thine eyes from tears: for thy work shall be rewarded, saith the Lord; and they shall come again from the land of the enemy. And there is hope in thine end."[31]

Providence is never too cloudy for hope to see fair weather coming from the promise.

Hope is an ointment that heals from a distance. The saints' hope is laid up in heaven, and yet it heals all the wounds they receive on earth.

But this is not all. As hope prophesies concerning the happy end of the Christian's afflictions, so it assures him he will be cared for while he endures them.[32]

Christian, you have no more effective argument to defeat temptation than your hope.

Hope's innocent argument will put you into a stronger tower against sin than all the sophisticated weapons of the uncircumcised world.[33]

"Hope's innocent argument." What poets the Puritans were as they wrestled with the hardest issues of practical spiritual life with the devices of biblical truth! But of course, they were also men and women of prayer, prayer that started and ended with hope.

Others in our own day have walked the same pathways and discovered the rich secrets of the connections between the two. For if hope is to be more than just a developed personality trait or a conditioned habit of thought, then it must anchor the soul to God himself. We'll see in the final chapter just how this is done.

ELEVEN

The Fruits
of Hope

The stories of hope's wonderful—and at times surely supernatural— entry into the lives of ordinary people at crucial moments are as inspiring as they are diverse.

HOPE, BECAUSE GOD IS IN THE WORLD

Take Bill Beutel, who was on his way to play tennis when he was told that his college-age daughter had been involved in a serious car wreck. Bill had not hitherto been a man of prayer at all. Like many busy people suddenly caught up in the uncontrollable vortices of life, he wondered whether his very busyness even gave him the right to pray.

"I felt that prayer was the privilege of those who practiced faith ardently," he said later. "So as I sped along, all I could manage was a whispered cry that my child would live, and the flickering hope that Someone was listening."[1]

Someone *was* listening. Bill Beutel's daughter recovered fully and became happily married not long afterwards. Thinking back, her father realized that it was his "flickering hope" for her that had, in fact, become the cause of awaking his previously dormant faith.[2]

For Dorothy Dudley Muth, from Carlsbad, California, hope nested once more in her broken heart after she saw a beautiful and unexpected rainbow in the sky. She was by herself on one of those romantic catamaran rides off Hawaii, with the rest of the passengers seemingly paired off contentedly and romantically with each other.

Her husband had insisted on a divorce; anger and self-pity gnawed at her from inside. But the brilliant display of sunshine and rain broke into this gloom. "As I watched the colors brighten," she later wrote,

167

I remembered the rainbow that God gave as a sign of his covenant with Noah.... I knew the double rainbow held great significance for me. If I put my life in His hands, He would not abandon me. His mercy would help heal my grief. As the Leahi came about to sail back, the waters shimmered gold from the setting sun. And I knew there was hope in my life again.[3]

California-based writer Lela Gilbert had suffered most of her childhood from a serious skin disease that responded to no form of medical treatment. The appearance was mortifying for an adolescent girl, and the constant itching a humiliating and often frightening reminder of the condition. At a Billy Graham crusade in Los Angeles in 1963, she went forward to give her life to Jesus Christ.

Four years after her commitment to Christ, she was walking down the street in Los Angeles when the thought came to her with overpowering conviction: God wanted to heal her. She told her mother who, perhaps out of a desire to protect her from disappointment, thoughtlessly commented: "Well, just don't get your hopes up."

But Lela did get her hopes up—and was healed so totally that she went on to become a fashion model. Lela says that she learned three things from the experience: "To get up and get going, no matter how painful the circumstances, and to show compassion to the diseased and despairing." Then, she adds, "One other thing I will never forget: it's all right to get my hopes up, when God is in the world."[4]

Very often, hope can be like a flag planted in the enemy territory of discouragement and doubt, a rallying point for renewed faith and boldness. Even the word *hope*, defiantly employed in the name of an organization or project, can bring about victory. One of the fastest-growing churches in Asia, and perhaps the world is called, simply, Hope of Bangkok Church. Under its pastor, Kriengsak Charoenwongsak, the church by the early 1990s had grown from nothing to six thousand members, overflowing with worshipers in a former movie theater five times each Sunday, and helping plant seventy-five daughter-churches around Thailand.

What is especially poignant about Hope of Bangkok's success is that missionaries traditionally regarded Bangkok, whose population is devoutly Buddhist, as "hopeless" for Christian evangelism. Of course there are numerous other instances of the name *hope* inspiring courageous projects:

"Plant Seeds of Hope" is a fundraising campaign to help retarded citizens.

"City of Hope" (Medical Research), based in Duarte, California, is an organization seeking to nurture medical breakthroughs in several fields.

"Restoring Hope Through Educational and Medical Aid" in Fort Lauderdale is a group helping to improve the quality of life in Haiti.

HOPE IN IMPRISONMENT

Lela Gilbert's advice to show compassion to the diseased and despairing had itself been followed by one of the most remarkable practitioners of hope in the twentieth century. The Austrian-born psychologist Viktor Frankl mesmerized the world with his book *Man's Search for Meaning,* first published in German just one year after World War II was over, but in English in 1959.

Frankl survived the Dantean inferno of Nazi death camps and wrote one of the most insightful accounts ever composed on how to cope with captivity and deprivation. His story is especially poignant in its frank explanation of why some prisoners somehow managed to come through the concentration camp experience to the end of the war and others simply gave up on the desire to live and died. At one point, he explains:

> The prisoner who had lost faith in the future—his future—was doomed. With his loss of belief in the future, he also lost his spiritual hold; he let himself decline and became subject to mental and physical decay. Usually this happened quite suddenly, in the form of a crisis, the symptoms of which were familiar to the experienced camp inmate.[5]

Long before the confirming findings of modern medicine about the relationship of hope to physical survival, especially after surgery or physical trauma of any kind, Frankl wrote:

> Those who know how close the connection is between the state of mind of a man—his courage and hope, or lack of them—and the state of immunity of his body will understand that the sudden loss of hope and courage can have a deadly effect.[6]

Frankl was not talking theoretically: A close friend in the camp quite simply died of disappointment that he would not be released, though it was just days before the camp was liberated by the Allies. So important did hope become for the prisoners that at one point both the senior block warden and Frankl himself spoke urgently about it to an assembled group of prisoners on a day when the authorities had withheld food as collective punishment for some potatoes that had been stolen. He explained candidly that many of the recent deaths among the prisoners might have resulted directly from their having given up hope. Frankl went on with his description:

> Whoever was still alive had reason to hope. Health, family, happiness, professional abilities, fortune, position in society—all these were things that could be achieved again or restored.... I asked the poor creatures who listened to me attentively in the darkness of the hut to face up to the seriousness of our position. They must not lose hope but should keep their courage in the certainty that the hopelessness of our struggle did not detract from its dignity and its meaning.[7]

Hope has been so recurrent a theme in accounts by prisoners of their experience in different kinds of incarceration that its usage in prison literature—and even advertising—has become almost intuitive. When Columbia Pictures released *The Shawshank Redemption,* a dramatic story of a strong friendship in a brutally run prison, the one-page, full-color advertisement for the movie in many magazines was inscribed with the heading, "Fear can hold you prisoner. Hope can set you free."

F *ear can hold you prisoner.*
  Hope can set you free.

One of the last major accounts of life in the Soviet gulag was by the poet Irina Ratushinskaya and entitled *Grey Is the Color of Hope.* The topic of hope is not discussed directly in the book at all, but one passage helps explain the title:

> I treasure my old zek (prisoner) uniform, made by Pani Lida, even though it means nothing to anyone here. And at times I pull out this camp "skin," which has seen so much, and press it to my cheek: grey, my very own grey color! The color of hope![8]

Another "hope" of a harrowing story of brutality in a Communist prison was written by Cuban poet Armando Vallodares and entitled *Against All Hope.*[9]

Commenting on this hope-oriented characteristic of worldwide prison literature, Jurgen Moltman recalled his own three years as a prisoner of war during World War II. Reading Dostoyevski, he said, had first showed him "how to suffer and to hope in and with the people." The imprisonment itself, he said, had provided the seedbed for his own "theology of hope." Yet that aspiration, or expectation, to be more accurate, didn't derive from the common and predictable desire of all prisoners to be free. "Rather," Moltman has asserted,

Hope came to life as the prisoner accepted his imprisonment, affirmed the barbed wire, and in this situation discovered the real human being in himself and others. It was not at his release but even while in prison that the "resurrection from the dead" happened for him. Faith inside "the house of the dead" is resurrection faith, as Dostoyevski continually emphasizes.[10]

"A FREEDOM NO MAN CAN TOUCH"

Nowhere has the truth of this insight been more powerfully demonstrated than in China, where thousands of Chinese Christians suffered years of brutality and torture in Communist prisons from the 1950s onward, solely on account of their Christian faith. Workers of East Gates Ministries International, a Washington State-based ministry to China's Christians, have met many Chinese believers after their release from prison. One such believer made an indelible impression on an East Gates representative when the two met.

Wang Chenliang (not his real name) had survived twenty years in prison and was now an old man, bent in body and wrinkled. What was it about him that caused him to exude a sense of emotional and psychological wholeness more vibrant than that of virtually any Westerner? The East Gates worker knew that many Chinese Christians had cracked under the pressure and become informers.

"God put me in school there," Wang replied. "I learned to give up my rights." He went on:

The Bible doesn't always guarantee we will always live in freedom, does it? No! So I learned to give up my "right" to freedom. I learned to give up my "right" to live with my family too. And I gave up my "right" to earn my way and accumulate wealth. In fact, the only right I could find in the Bible was my right to be a child of God. That one I did not give up! So, you see, once I learned to give up these things, I became a free man. When you have died to self, you discover a freedom no man can touch.[11]

Wang had discovered one of the most important ingredients of all prayer, the willingness to release into the hands of God the very thing that you are praying most earnestly for. Paradoxically, this kind of "abandonment" is also the very key to maintaining in your life a hope that does not depend on circumstances but always looks beyond to God himself who holds all circumstances in his hand.

Another Christian who spent years in Communist prison camps and while there came to a Christian faith is the Nobel Prize-winning Russian writer Alexander Solzhenitsyn. Many believe that Solzhenitsyn's relentlessly detailed exposure of the vast wickedness of the Soviet gulag, the sprawling, continent-wide archipelago of forced labor camps, contributed significantly to the collapse of Communism in the Soviet Union itself.

Late in 1993, Solzhenitsyn reflected on the perils that continue to face the human race even after global Communism has ceased to be a threat to peace and freedom. After looking back on the appalling human cost of the entire Communist experiment in Russia, China, and other countries of the world, Solzhenitsyn wrote:

And yet, surely we have not experienced the trials of the 20th century in vain. Let us hope. We have, after all, been tempered by these trials and our hard-won firmness will in some fashion be passed on to the following generations.[12]

Some may question how deeply the lessons of the twentieth century's battle with the totalitarian temptation have been absorbed, particularly given the post-Communist bloodletting in former Yugoslavia, the chaos and brutality in many parts of Africa, and the rise of Islamic radicalist terrorism. Yet Solzhenitsyn's hope is anchored on the right foundation: the knowledge that it is in neither man's noblest nor his meanest abilities that true hope for the human race resides. It was on the misguided basis of an idolatry of man's wisdom that Communism and its Teutonic rival, Nazism, arose in the first place.

For most people, it is nevertheless the hope for change just beyond their reach rather than over the horizon of history that illuminates their daily living with joy and determination that inspire all around them. One of the best-liked workers at the Christian Broadcasting Network in Chesapeake, Virginia, is an outgoing, vibrantly energetic African-American called Doug Warner.

OUR UNQUENCHABLE HOPE

Doug, fifty-five, is a talented jazz musician as well as a busy and effective coordinator of the many prominent guests who fly into Norfolk to be on *The 700 Club*. Yet as he was growing up in Petersburg, Virginia, he had to cope with life in an area of town infested with cockroaches and a racism as casual as it was endemic. Did these adverse circumstances deter Doug Warner from envisioning, and then hoping for (expecting) a way of life that was full of fun and dignity? Let Doug answer the question himself:

> Hope to me was a chance. It was a sense that there was nothing I couldn't do. I had a grandmother who was very religious who told me that I could make it, if I was polite, decent. I was taught to be a clean-cut young person. We were poor, but I didn't know it because I was rich in so much character and integrity. Hope was real to me because the principles my grandmother taught me were valid. I can't imagine a child not having hope.[13]

A vital ingredient in the hope of people like Doug Warner is an entirely legitimate desire for change. The divine hope implanted within Christians fills them with a restlessness about the fallen nature of the world into which they are born and which is permeated with the fallenness of generations before them. As Moltman explains:

> That we do not reconcile ourselves, that there is no pleasant harmony between us and reality, is due to our unquenchable hope. This hope keeps man unreconciled, until the great day of the fulfillment of all the

promises of God.... This hope makes the Christian Church a constant disturbance in human society, seeking as the latter does to stabilize itself into a "continuing city."... Thus it will constantly arouse the "passion for the possible," inventiveness and elasticity in self-transformation, in breaking the old and coming to terms with the new.[14]

This aspect of hope as a dynamic that sets things in motion has been noted by many people, both identifiably Christian and not overtly religious at all. The *New Catholic Encyclopedia* says that the "act of hope is dynamic, energizing the will most efficaciously and putting right order in its relation to the means."[15]

The late Senator Robert F. Kennedy, speaking at the Day of Affirmation Address at the University of Capetown in South Africa, two years to the day before his own tragic death by an assassin's bullet, compared hope to the tiny, but in the end powerful, movement of water in a pond. "Each time a man stands up for an ideal," he told an audience still bound by the restrictions of apartheid,

or acts to improve the lot of others, or strikes out against injustice, he sends forth a tiny ripple of hope, and crossing each other from a million different centers of energy and daring, those ripples build a current which can sweep down the mightiest walls of oppression and resistance.[16]

Though Kennedy himself was cut down in the prime of his life, those ripples of which he spoke had smashed down the walls of apartheid eighteen years later, and gave South Africans of all races a chance to hope for a truly multiracial society open to all. It is true that many skeptics have voiced worry about the ability of whites, coloreds, and blacks to devise a system that would lessen economic disparities among the races without undermining other structures vital for a flourishing democracy and economy. Yet the existence of widespread hope among all races at the beginning of black majority rule in South Africa in 1994 could scarcely have been imagined when Robert Kennedy spoke.

HOW CAN WE PRAY WITH HOPE?

How do Christians find hope? It's important to recognize first that hope is not a quality or a virtue that comes only to those who are famous writers in prison or Christian pastors persecuted for their faith. Hope has to be a day-to-day, commonplace virtue or most people will give up on attempting to cultivate it and apply it in their lives.

"Hope can be an 'Everyman's virtue,'" says Michele Clark, a professional worker in Washington, D.C., "and clinging to hope is part of everyman's heroism." She explains further,

> Ultimately, the things I hope for include: the hope of being known and accepted for who I am, the hope that my life will count for something, the hope of "belonging," and having a place somewhere, the need to know that "all is not lost," and that the horrible things I have done will not forever be counted against me, or keep me from achieving the noble things I somehow keep finding within my own heart and spirit.[17]

How, therefore, do you get hope? "Why, you practice it in the way you practice any skill you want to master," says Norman Vincent Peale. He explains:

> As you go through the day, plant little seeds of hope in other people. A friend is facing a difficulty? Tell him you feel sure he is equal to it. A student is nervous and fearful about an oncoming exam? Tell him you feel sure he is equal to it. Your expectancy will rub off on him. Scientific scholastic studies have shown that if a teacher expects a child to do well in class, chances are greatly improved that the child will do well. Why? How? Because the teacher's expectancy transmits hope, and hope makes achievement easier.[18]

It's important to note that Peale does not conceive of hope as a virtue in the abstract. It is rooted, for him, in the Christian's relationship with God. He goes on:

> I have lived a long time now and have known and observed many people through the years. And I maintain that the nearer a person comes to the Savior, the more hope he or she has. You just cannot live

with Jesus Christ and be defeated or depressed. You cannot live with Him and say, "Tomorrow is not going to be any good." Because, He is the Lord of the tomorrows.... Remember, you do not go into the New Year alone, but with the loving God Who has walked with you ever since you were a child. So light the flame of hope and watch the shadows vanish.[19]

Hope is thus linked inseparably with faith, and the two of them are designed to operate hand in hand with love, the Christian *agape*, just as Charles Péguy made clear so elegantly in his epic poem on hope. All three virtues are gifts of God, acts of grace which we receive. Having received them, moreover, we walk forward in them, we strengthen them, nourish them, until they provide us with powerful armaments for staying strong and courageous throughout life's challenges and for implanting these qualities in others.

H*ope can be an "Everyman's virtue," and clinging to hope is part of everyman's heroism.*

SIX STEPS TO INCREASED HOPE

William Gurnall, our Puritan friend, has additional practical advice on how to make one's hope even stronger.

First, study the Word of God diligently
Secondly, keep a pure conscience
Thirdly, ask God for a stronger hope
Fourthly, increase your love
Fifthly, exercise your hope, and
Sixthly, recall past mercies.[20]

Both the first and the sixth points in this advice are essential keys to the building up of hope. One reason we read God's Word, the Bible, as one remarkable student of the Bible has written, "is to get to know the author of the book. Knowing the author of the Bible is the most important thing in life."[21]

One reason for knowing the Bible is to understand what God promises to those who seek to follow him through Jesus Christ. The list is quite impressive: eternal life, healing, peace, joy, forgiveness, strength, power to love, to name but the most obvious. All of the promises, in fact, are related to hope, and the better acquainted we are with the promises, the stronger reason we will have for hope in all of our present circumstances.

> H*ope is thus linked inseparably with faith, and the two of them are designed to operate hand in hand with love.*

In addition, recalling "past mercies," gifts that God has placed in our lives in answer to prayer, or simply out of the blue, both reinforces our conviction of God's goodness and reaffirms the power of the promises themselves. As Gurnall explains:

> God's promises are hope's substance to act upon. A man can as well live without air as faith and hope can live without a promise, and without taking in refreshment from that promise frequently.... And if you are a wise Christian you will not be satisfied merely to think about God's promises now and then while you are preoccupied but will find a place apart and enjoy meditating on them.[22]

Gurnall adds some further advice on how to find hope when we have become deeply discouraged, or when all of the standard rallying cries of Christian strength do not seem to help us. With the great sense of practicality that the Puritans so often showed, Gurnall makes the analogy of a hound that has temporarily lost the scent in the chase, just as we may temporarily have lost the dynamic for going forward in our Christian walk:

> When a hound has lost the scent, he hunts backward to recover it and pursues his game with a louder cry of confidence than before. Thus, Christian, when your hope is at a loss and you question your salvation in another world, look backward to see what God has done for you in this one.... Past experiences with God are a sure foundation for hope in future hardships and also a powerful argument in prayer.... So you should not only feast with the joy of mercy but save the remembrance of it as hope-seed, to strengthen you to wait on God for further mercy and help in time of need.[23]

Gurnall's other points among the six should not be overlooked, either. Norman Vincent Peale was cited earlier on how to get hope by giving it away. But the "pure conscience" and "increase your love" aspects of hope are no less important. Purity of heart and mind are essential ingredients in a successful Christian life under all circumstances, but they are uniquely necessary for the joyful residence of hope in our hearts. Our hope, after all, comes from heaven, and heavenly things do not like to reside in unclean vessels. Gurnall, as usual, says it most eloquently:

> Living godly in this present world and "looking for that blessed hope" are joined together (Ti 2:12-13). Thus a soul void of godliness must be destitute of all true hope, and the godly person who is careless in his holy walk will soon find his hope faltering.[24]

Similarly, Gurnall reminds us, "Love has a secret influence on hope.... It is fear that oppresses the Christian's spirit so that he cannot act or hope strongly. "Perfect love casteth out fear" (1 Jn 4:18).[25]

HOPE AND PRAYER

But action and attitude are only one part of hope. No less important is the vital relationship of all hope to effective prayer. Josef Pieper, whose insights into the Christian understanding of hope we looked at in an earlier chapter, has said that prayer, "in its original form as a prayer of petition, is nothing other than the voicing of hope." Pieper reinforces this view by reminding us of the Lord's instructions to his disciples "always to pray and not lose heart" (Lk 18:1).[26]

Henri Nouwen, whose reflections on prayer are fine examples of devotional writing, expresses the same idea. "Every prayer," he says, "is an expression of hope. A man who expects nothing from the future cannot pray.... For this man, life stands still."[27] He adds, "The important thing about prayer is not whether it is classified as petition, thanksgiving, or praise, but whether it is a prayer of hope or of little faith."[28]

Another way of putting it is that all prayer must be prayer of expectation, an orientation toward God that demonstrates certainty not only about God's goodness but about his total and undivided attentiveness toward his children. It must not be a carping, whiny, complaining kind of prayer—how open are any of us to the bleatings of a bad-tempered and demanding child?—but prayer that is at one and the same time expectant and open to the Holy Spirit.

"In the silence of prayer," Nouwen explains, "you can spread out your hands to embrace nature, God, and your fellowman. This acceptance not only means that you are ready to look at your own limitations, but that you expect the coming of something new."[29]

How legitimate is it to hope in prayer for the things one genuinely desires? In one sense, it is totally legitimate. Our understanding of God from the Bible is that he cares for his children and delights to give us the desires of our hearts (Ps 37:4). Does that mean that he always gives each Christian each and every desire put forward in prayer? Of course not.

Just as a child's requests of a parent, even if offered quietly and humbly, are not always answered affirmatively—because the child is often unaware of conflicting circumstances that are known to a wise parent—so our own prayer requests, couched though they may be in hope, cannot always be affirmatively answered by our heavenly Father. Nouwen is quite open about this. "For the prayer of hope," he says,

> ...it is essential that there are no guarantees asked, no conditions posed, and no proofs demanded, only that you expect everything from the other without binding him in any way. Hope is based on the premise that the other gives only what is good.[30]

The late Catherine Marshall thought long and hard about the paradox of praying in hope (in her case of a physical healing) when it appeared that her pleading, importunate petitions to God to intervene and heal were getting nowhere. Finally, she came to the conclusion that the way she needed to pray was to admit that she had been badgering God in prayer and had not fully declared to him that she would trust him no matter what happened. One day, she prayed what she later called "the prayer of relinquishment," an admission to God that she would gratefully accept whatever came from his hand. She was instantly healed.

Catherine Marshall had, of course, "hoped" to be healed—that is, she earnestly desired to be healed though she wasn't completely sure that God would do so. But the hope in which she prayed, by her own account, was evidently not the hope of total trust, the hope that is anchored in heaven for us. This hope alone is totally authentic, because it depends not on our desires, much less on the "rights" that we are sometimes encouraged to believe we can employ to manipulate God, but on God's promises.

"Even with hope," she once explained, "our relinquishment must be the real thing, because this giving up of self-will is the hardest thing we human beings are ever called on to do."[31]

HOPE IN THE MIDST OF SUFFERING

For many Christians hope seems especially hard to grasp because they are in the midst of great suffering. How, in those circumstances, are we supposed to hope? Suppose, somehow, not even William Gurnall's six points for strengthening help seem to work? A great twentieth-century Protestant thinker comes to our aid here, our old friend Eugene Petersen. "A Christian is a person who decides to face and live through suffering," he says bluntly. "If we do not make that decision, we are endangered on every side."[32]

But how do we acquire hope and live in it if we are so beleaguered by our circumstances we can scarcely keep our heads above water? Petersen's answer is to look at Psalm 130, where the psalmist, in the midst of terrible travail (we are not told its nature in the psalm), sees his way out of the pain and the present by attending upon God as a watchman attends upon the coming of the morning. "I wait for the Lord, my soul waits, and in his word I put my hope. My soul waits for the Lord more than watchmen wait for the morning, more than watchmen wait for the morning" (Ps 130:5-6).

"There is more than a description of reality here, there is a procedure for participating in it," says Petersen, who describes in his book his own experiences as a nightwatchman early in his life. He elaborates:

A watchman is an important person, but he doesn't do very much.... He knows the dawn is coming; there are no doubts concerning that. Meanwhile he is alert to the dangers, he comforts restless children or animals until it is time to work or play again in the light of day.... Waiting does not mean doing nothing. It is not fatalistic resignation. It means going about our assigned tasks, confident that God will provide the meaning and the conclusions. It is not compelled to work away at keeping up appearances with bogus spirituality. It is the opposite of desperate and panicky manipulations, of scurrying and worrying.[33]

"HOPE MEANS TO KEEP LIVING"

What a vigorous, open-hearted, confident approach to hope amid turmoil. No doubt with experience behind him—and how many Christians have not encountered at least a little of this?—he notes that "when we suffer, we attract counselors as money attracts thieves" and tend to get flooded "first with sympathy and then with advice. But none of that is what we need," Petersen insists. "We need hope. We need to know that we are in relation to God. We need to know that suffering is part of what it means to be human and not something alien."[34]

To wait and hope. Surely the key to all hope that is anchored into heaven for us by God's promises involves waiting, for no matter how carefully we may plan—and we emphatically should plan—our times are never finally in our own hands. The moments of providence, moreover, correspond very seldom to our own notions of how the world should turn.

Hope can be compared to many quite different things. Hope is like the domestic cat that will not come when called but nestles affectionately up to us when we least expect her to.

Hope is like the anchor that holds the ship in place—the ship biblically being our own soul—no matter how much the storm rages around us and tries to tug us free.

Hope is like the lion in the forest, triumphant over all the animals, patient, never hurried, always king of his domain. Hope should clearly be these things to us, and many others. As Nouwen so eloquently wrote,

> Hope means to keep living
>   amid desperation,
>   and to keep humming in darkness.
> Hoping is knowing that there is love,
>   it is trust in tomorrow
>   it is falling asleep
>   and waking again
>   when the sun rises.
> In the midst of a gale at sea,
>   it is to discover land.
> In the eyes of another
>   it is to see that he understands you.

As long as there is still hope
    there will also be prayer.
And God will be holding you
    in his hands.[35]

HOPE'S PERSONAL MIRACLE

But what of my own search for hope? How had that proceeded? Once my searching was complete, was hope, for me, still just a "drunkard's condolence"? Oh no. In no way.

Yes, the Old Testament did have some answers; and the New Testament; and the reflections of saintly men and women of God across the centuries; and a deeper conviction than ever before of the fundamental truth of the Christian faith.

But more than anything else, as I threaded my way through the pathways of hope within the Jewish and Christian traditions and the landscapes of other faiths, God's grace reached down and reassembled hope in my own life. He did so, first of all, by entering into the greatest of my catastrophes, the broken-down structure of my marriage. He reassembled this structure in a new, more wonderful way than I had ever imagined possible.

Without any of the present-day paraphernalia of counselors, mediators, psychologists, or therapists that is assumed by some to be essential before God can do his work, his grace worked a remarkable change in my heart and my wife's toward each other. Even our family and our closest friends were amazed at what they saw happening in front of them.

Many had heard our separate complaints about the reasons for our relationship's collapse. The explanations each of us had offered had been entirely rational, and by the world's standards, not unreasonable. Yet man's reasonableness is always less powerful than God's mercy and forgiveness. Before this book was completed, both my wife and I were delightedly reunited in one home with our children, and with a new sense of what God had in store for us. Ours was a completely new hope.

Nor did the healing cease there. My two daughters seemed to find not just a new joy in life at their parents' new happiness but a new conviction in their own lives that the God of hope is truly just that. With that conviction came their own new dedication, a sense that God's calling is never a static requisition upon our lives but always a summons. He calls us toward him, of course, but also out of ourselves, into the world—and into hope.

Old Testament Citations of Hope

Return home, my daughters; I am too old to have another husband. Even if I thought there was still hope for me—even if I had a husband tonight and then gave birth to sons — would you wait until they grew up?

Ruth 1:12-13

We are aliens and strangers in your sight, as were all our forefathers. Our days on earth are like a shadow, without hope. **1 Chronicles 29:15**

Then Shecaniah son of Jehiel, one of the descendants of Elam, said to Ezra, "We have been unfaithful to our God by marrying foreign women from the peoples around us. But in spite of this, there is still hope for Israel." **Ezra 10:2**

Should not your piety be your confidence and your blameless ways your hope? **Job 4:6**

So the poor have hope, and injustice shuts its mouth.

Job 5:16

Oh, that I might have my request, that God would grant what I hope for, that God would be willing to crush me, to let loose his hand and cut me off! **Job 6:8-9**

What strength do I have, that I should still hope? **Job 6:11**

The caravans of Tema look for water, the traveling merchants of Sheba look in hope. **Job 6:19**

My days are swifter than a weaver's shuttle, and they come to an end without hope. **Job 7:6**

Such is the destiny of all who forget God; so perishes the hope of the godless. **Job 8:13**

You will be secure, because there is hope; you will look about you and take your rest in safety. **Job 11:18**

But the eyes of the wicked will fail, and escape will elude them; their hope will become a dying gasp. **Job 11:20**

Though he slay me, yet will I hope in him; I will surely defend my ways to his face. **Job 13:15**

At least there is hope for a tree: If it is cut down, it will sprout again, and its new shoots will not fail. **Job 14:7**

But as a mountain erodes and crumbles and as a rock is moved from its place, as water wears away stones and torrents wash away the soil, so you destroy man's hope. **Job 14:18-19**

If the only home I hope for is the grave, if I spread out my bed in darkness, if I say to corruption, "You are my father," and to the worm, "My mother" or "My sister," where then is my hope? Who can see any hope for me? **Job 17:13-15**

He tears me down on every side till I am gone; he uproots my hope like a tree. **Job 19:10**

For what hope has the godless when he is cut off, when God takes away his life? **Job 27:8**

Any hope of subduing him (a hippopotamus, or an elephant) is false; the mere sight of him is overpowering. **Job 41:9**

But the needy will not always be forgotten, nor the hope of the afflicted ever perish. **Psalm 9:18**

No one whose hope is in you will ever be put to shame, but they will be put to shame who are treacherous without excuse. **Psalm 25:3**

Show me your ways, O Lord, teach me your paths; guide me in your truth and teach me, for you are God my Savior, and my hope is in you all day long. **Psalm 25:4-5**

May integrity and uprightness protect me, because my hope is in you. **Psalm 25:21**

Be strong and take heart, all you who hope in the Lord. **Psalm 31:24**

A horse is a vain hope for deliverance; despite all its great strength it cannot save. But the eyes of the Lord are on those who fear him, on those whose hope is in his unfailing love, to deliver them from death and keep them alive in famine. We wait in hope for the Lord; he is our help and our shield. In him our hearts rejoice, for we trust in his holy name. May your unfailing love rest upon us, O Lord, even as we put our hope in you. **Psalm 33:17-22**

For evil men will be cut off, but those who hope in the Lord will inherit the land. **Psalm 37:9**

But now, Lord, what do I look for? My hope is in you. **Psalm 39:7**

Why are you downcast, O my soul? Why so disturbed within me? Put your hope in God, for I will yet praise him, my Savior and my God. **Psalm42:5-6**

I will praise you forever for what you have done; in your name I will hope, for your name is good. I will praise you in the presence of the saints. **Psalm 52:9**

Find rest, O my soul, in God alone; my hope comes from him. **Psalm 62:5**

You answer us with awesome deeds of righteousness, O God our Savior, the hope of all the ends of the earth and of the farthest seas, who formed the mountains by your power, having armed yourself with strength, who stilled the roaring of the seas, the roaring of their waves, and the turmoil of the nations.   **Psalm 65:5-7**

May those who hope in you not be disgraced because of me, O God of Israel.   **Psalm 69:6**

For you have been my hope, O Sovereign Lord, my confidence since my youth.   **Psalm 71:5**

But as for me, I will always have hope; I will praise you more and more.
                                                                    Psalm 71:14

Do not snatch the word of truth from my mouth, for I have put my hope in your laws.   **Psalm 119:43**

Remember your word to your servant, for you have given me hope.
                                                                   Psalm 119:49

May they who fear you rejoice when they see me, for I have put my hope in your word.   **Psalm 119:74**

My soul faints with longing for your salvation, for I have put my hope in your word.   **Psalm 119:81**

You are my refuge and my shield; I have put my hope in your word.
                                                                  Psalm 119:114

I rise before dawn and cry for help; I have put my hope in your word.
                                                                  Psalm 119:147

I wait for the Lord, my soul waits, and in his word I have put my hope.
                                                                   Psalm 130:5

O Israel, put your hope in the Lord, for with the Lord is unfailing love and with him is full redemption.   **Psalm 130:7**

O Israel, put your hope in the Lord both now and for evermore.
                                                                   Psalm 131:3

Blessed is he whose help is the God of Jacob, whose hope is in the Lord his God, the Maker of heaven and earth, the sea, and everything in them—the Lord, who remains faithful for ever. **Psalm 146:5**

His pleasure is not in the strength of the horse, nor his delight in the legs of a man; the Lord delights in those who fear him, who put their hope in his unfailing love. **Psalm 147:10-11**

When a wicked man dies, his hope perishes; all he expected from his power comes to nothing. **Proverbs 11:7**

The desire of the righteous ends only in good, but the hope of the wicked only in wrath. **Proverbs 11:23**

Hope deferred makes the heart sick, but a longing fulfilled is a tree of life. **Proverbs 13:12**

Discipline your son, for in that there is hope; do not be a willing party to his death. **Proverbs 19:18**

There is surely a future hope for you, and your hope will not be cut off. **Proverbs 23:18**

Know also that wisdom is sweet to your soul; if you find it, there is a future hope for you, and your hope will not be cut off. **Proverbs 24:14**

For the evil man has no future hope, and the lamp of the wicked will be snuffed out. **Proverbs 24:20**

Do you see a man wise in his own eyes? There is more hope for a fool than for him. **Proverbs 26:12**

Do you see a man who speaks in haste? There is more hope for a fool than for him. **Proverbs 29:20**

Anyone who is among the living has hope—even a live dog is better off than a dead lion! **Ecclesiastes 9:4**

Those who work with combed flax will despair, the weavers of fine linen will lose hope. **Isaiah 19:9**

For the grave cannot praise you, death cannot sing your praise; those who go down to the pit cannot hope for your faithfulness. **Isaiah 19:9**

Even youths grow tired and weary, and young men stumble and fall, but those who hope in the Lord will renew their strength. They will soar on wings like eagles, they will run and not grow weary, they will walk and not be faint. **Isaiah 40:30-31**

In faithfulness he will bring forth justice; he will not falter or be discouraged till he establishes justice on earth. In his law the islands will put their hope. **Isaiah 42:3-4**

Then you will know that I am the Lord; those who hope in me will not be disappointed. **Isaiah 49:23**

The islands will look to me and wait in hope for my arm. **Isaiah 51:5**

Give glory to the Lord your God before he brings the darkness, before your feet stumble on the darkening hills. You hope for light, but he will turn it to thick darkness and change it to deep gloom. **Jeremiah 13:16**

O hope of Israel, its Savior in times of distress, why are you like a stranger in the land, like a traveler who stays only a night? **Jeremiah 14:8**

No, it is you, O Lord our God. Therefore our hope is in you, for you are the one who does all this. **Jeremiah 14:22**

O Lord, the hope of Israel, all who forsake you will be put to shame.
Jeremiah 17:13

"For I know the plans I have for you," declares the Lord, "plans to prosper you and not to harm you, plans to give you a hope and a future."
Jeremiah 29:11

"So there is a hope for your future," declares the Lord.   **Jeremiah 31:17**

Whoever found them devoured them; their enemies said, "We are not guilty, for they sinned against the Lord, their true pasture, the hope of their fathers."   **Jeremiah 50:7**

Yet this I call to mind and therefore I have hope.   **Lamentations 3:21**

The Lord is good to those whose hope is in him, to the one who seeks him; it is good to wait quietly for the salvation of the Lord.
                                                          Lamentations 3:25-26

Let him bury his face in the dust—there may yet be hope.
                                                          Lamentations 3:29

When she saw her hope unfulfilled, her expectation gone, she took another of her cubs and made him a strong lion.   **Ezekiel 19:5**

Then he said to me: "Son of man, these bones are the whole house of Israel. They say, 'Our bones are dried up and our hope is gone; we are cut off.'"   **Ezekiel 37:11**

There I will give her back her vineyards, and will make the Valley of Achor a door of hope.   **Hosea 2:15**

But as for me, I watch in hope for the Lord, I wait for God my Savior; my God will hear me.   **Micah 7:7**

Ashkelon will see it and fear; Gaza will writhe in agony, and Ekron too, for her hope will wither.   **Zechariah 9:5**

Return to your fortress, O prisoners of hope; even now I announce that I will restore twice as much to you.   **Zechariah 9:12**

New Testament Citations of Hope

Note: When they do not denote direct speech, quotation marks in the citations below are quotations from the Old Testament.

The noun *hope* is not found at all in the Gospels and the verb only five times, in the sense of "to trust" (Matthew 12:21; John 5:45) or in a purely secular and nonreligious context (Luke 6:34; 23:8; 24:21).

In his name the nations will put their hope.   **Matthew 12:21**

A quotation from Isaiah 42:1-4, which reads, "In his law the islands will put their hope." In the Hebrew Scriptures the word *islands* usually referred to Gentile nations.

And if you lend to those from whom you expect repayment, what credit is that to you? Even "sinners" lend to "sinners," expecting to be repaid in full.   **Luke 6:34**

When Herod saw Jesus, he was greatly pleased, because for a long time he had been wanting to see him. From what he had heard about him, he hoped to see him perform some miracle.   **Luke 23:8**

The chief priests and our rulers handed him over to be sentenced to death, and they crucified him; but we had hoped that he was the one who was going to redeem Israel. And what is more, it is the third day since all this took place.   **Luke 24:20-21**

But do not think I will accuse you before the Father. Your accuser is Moses, on whom your hopes are set.   **John 5:45**

Therefore... my body also will live in hope, because you will not abandon me to the grave, nor will you let your Holy One see decay. **Acts 2:26-27**

A quotation from Psalm 16:8-11, which reads, "Therefore my heart is glad and my tongue rejoices; my body also will rest secure, because you will not abandon me to the grave, nor will you let your Holy One see decay."

When the owners of the slave girl realized that their hope of making money was gone, they seized Paul and Silas and dragged them into the marketplace to face the authorities. **Acts 16:19**

My brothers, I am a Pharisee, the son of a Pharisee. I stand on trial because of my hope in the resurrection of the dead. **Acts 23:6**

I believe everything that agrees with the Law and that is written in the Prophets, and I have the same hope in God as these men, that there will be a resurrection of both the righteous and the wicked. **Acts 24:14-15**

And now it is because of my hope in what God has promised our fathers that I am on trial today. **Acts 26:6**

When neither sun nor stars appeared for many days and the storm continued raging, we finally gave up all hope of being saved. **Acts 27:20**

For this reason I have asked to see you and talk with you. It is because of the hope of Israel that I am bound with this chain. **Acts 28:20**
*(This is a reference to the Jewish hope
in the coming of the Messiah.)*

Against all hope, Abraham in hope believed and so became the father of many nations, just as it had been said to him, "So shall your offspring be." **Romans 4:18**

And we rejoice in the hope of the glory of God. Not only so, but we also rejoice in our sufferings, because we know that suffering produces perseverance; perseverance, character; and character, hope. And hope does not disappoint us, because God has poured out his love into our hearts by the Holy Spirit, whom he has given us.   **Romans 5:2-5**

For the creation was subjected to frustration, not by its own choice, but by the will of the one who subjected it, in hope that the creation itself will be liberated from its bondage to decay and brought into the glorious freedom of the children of God.   **Romans 8:20-21**

For in this hope we were saved. But hope that is seen is no hope at all. Who hopes for what he already has? But if we hope for what we do not yet have, we wait for it patiently.   **Romans 8:24-25**

Inasmuch as I am the apostle to the Gentiles, I make much of my ministry in the hope that I may somehow arouse my own people to envy and save some of them.   **Romans 11:13-14**

Be joyful in hope, patient in affliction, faithful in prayer.   **Romans 12:12**

For everything that was written in the past was written to teach us, so that through endurance and the encouragement of the Scriptures, we might have hope.   **Romans 15:4**

The root of Jesse will spring up, one who will arise to rule over the nations; the Gentiles will hope in him.   **Romans 15:12**

    A quotation from Isaiah 11:10, which reads, "In that day the Root of Jesse will stand as a banner for the peoples; the nations will rally to him, and his place of rest will be glorious."

May the God of hope fill you with all joy and peace as you trust in him, so that you may overflow with hope by the power of the Holy Spirit.
                          Romans 15:13

I [plan] to visit you when I go to Spain. I hope to visit you while passing through and to have you assist me on my journey there, after I have enjoyed your company for a while.   **Romans 15:24**

Yes, this was written for us, because when the plowman ploughs and the thresher threshes, they ought to do so in the hope of sharing in the harvest. **1 Corinthians 9:10**

But I have not used any of these rights. And I am not writing this in the hope that you will do such things for me. **1 Corinthians 9:15**

And now these three remain: faith, hope and love. But the greatest of these is love. **1 Corinthians 13:13**

If only for this life we have hope in Christ, we are to be pitied more than all men. **1 Corinthians 15:19**

I hope to spend some time with you if the Lord permits.
1 Corinthians 16:7

And our hope for you is firm, because we know that just as you share in our sufferings, so also you share in our comfort. **2 Corinthians 1:7**

On him we have set our hope that he will continue to deliver us, as you help us by your prayers. **2 Corinthians 1:10-11**

And I hope that, as you have understood us in part, you will come to understand fully that you can boast of us just as we will boast of you in the day of the Lord Jesus. **2 Corinthians 1:13-14**

Therefore, since we have such a hope, we are very bold.
2 Corinthians 3:12

What we are is plain to God, and I hope it is also plain to your conscience.
2 Corinthians 5:11

Our hope is that, as your faith continues to grow, our area of activity among you will greatly expand, so that we can preach the gospel in the regions beyond you. **2 Corinthians 10:15-16**

I hope you will put up with a little of my foolishness; but you are already doing that. **2 Corinthians 11:1**

But by faith we eagerly await through the Spirit the righteousness for which we hope.   **Galatians 5:5**

In him we were also chosen, having been predestined according to the plan of him who works out everything in conformity with the purpose of his will, in order that we, who were the first to hope in Christ, might be for the praise of his glory.   **Ephesians 1:11-12**

I pray also that the eyes of your heart may be enlightened in order that you may know the hope to which he has called you, the riches of his glorious inheritance in the saints, and his incomparably great power for us who believe.   **Ephesians 1:18-19**

Remember that at that time you were separate from Christ, excluded from citizenship in Israel and foreigners to the covenants of the promise, without hope and without God in the world.   **Ephesians 2:12**

There is one body and one Spirit—just as you were called to one hope when you were called—one Lord, one faith, one baptism; one God and Father of all, who is over all and through all and in all.   **Ephesians 4:4-6**

I eagerly expect and hope that I will in no way be ashamed, but will have sufficient courage so that now as always Christ will be exalted in my body, whether by life or by death.   **Philippians 1:20**

I hope in the Lord Jesus to send Timothy to you soon, that I also may be cheered when I receive news about you.   **Philippians 2:19**

I hope, therefore, to send him as soon as I see how things go with me.
                                                                 Philippians 2:23

We always thank God, the Father of our Lord Jesus Christ, when we pray for you, because we have heard of your faith in Christ Jesus and of the love you have for all the saints—the faith and love that spring from the HOPE that is stored up for you in heaven and that you have already heard about in the word of truth, the gospel that has come to you.
                                                                  Colossians 1:3-6

But now he has reconciled you by Christ's physical body through death to present you holy in his sight, without blemish and free from accusation—if you continue in your faith, established and firm, not moved from the hope held out in the Gospel.   **Colossians 1:22-23**

To them God has chosen to make known amoung the Gentiles the glorious riches of this mystery, which is Christ in you, the hope of glory.
                                                          Colossians 1:27

We continually remember before our God and Father your work produced by faith, your labor prompted by love, and your endurance inspired by hope in our Lord Jesus Christ.   **1 Thessalonians 1:3**

For what is our hope, our joy, or the crown in which we will glory in the presence of our Lord Jesus Christ when he comes? Is it not you?
                                                          1 Thessalonians 2:19

Brothers, we do not want you to be ignorant about those who fall asleep, or to grieve like the rest of men, who have no hope.
                                                          1 Thessalonians 4:13

But since we belong to the day, let us be self-controlled, putting on faith and love as a breastplate, and the hope of salvation as a helmet.
                                                          1 Thessalonians 5:8

May our Lord Jesus Christ himself and God our Father, who loved us and by his grace gave us eternal encouragement and good hope, encourage your hearts and strengthen you in every good deed and word.
                                                          2 Thessalonians 2:16-17

Paul, an apostle of Christ Jesus by the command of God our Savior and of Christ Jesus our hope, to Timothy my true son in the faith: Grace, mercy and peace from God the Father and Christ Jesus our Lord.
                                                          1 Timothy 1:1-2

Although I hope to come to you soon, I am writing you these instructions so that, if I am delayed, you will know how people ought to conduct themselves in God's household, which is the church of the living God, the pillar and foundation of the truth.   **1 Timothy 3:14-15**

This is a trustworthy saying that deserves full acceptance (and for this we labor and strive), that we have put our hope in the living God, who is the Savior of all men, and especially of those who believe.   **1 Timothy 4:10**

The widow who is really in need and left all alone puts her hope in God and continues night and day to pray and to ask God for help.

1 Timothy 5:5

Command those who are rich in this present world not to be arrogant nor to put their hope in wealth, which is so uncertain, but to put their hope in God, who richly provides us with everything for our enjoyment.

1 Timothy 6:17

Those who oppose him he must gently instruct, in the hope that God will grant them repentance leading them to a knowledge of the truth and that they will come to their senses and escape from the trap of the devil, who has taken them captive to do his will.   **2 Timothy 2:25-26**

Paul, a servant of God and an apostle of Jesus Christ for the faith of God's elect and the knowledge of the truth that leads to godliness—a faith and knowledge resting on the hope of eternal life, which God, who does not lie, promised before the beginning of time, and at his appointed season he brought his word to light through the preaching entrusted to me by the command of God our Savior,
      To Titus, my true son in our command faith:
      Grace and peace from God the Father and Christ Jesus our Savior.

Titus 1:1-4

It [grace] teaches us to say "No" to ungodliness and worldly passions, and to live self-controlled, upright and godly lives in this present age, while we wait for the blessed hope—the glorious appearing of our great God and Savior, Jesus Christ, who gave himself for us to redeem us from all wickedness and to purify for himself a people that are his very own, eager to do what is good.   **Titus 2:12-14**

He saved us through the washing of rebirth and renewal by the Holy Spirit, whom he poured out on us generously through Jesus Christ our Savior, so that, having been justified by his grace, we might become heirs having the hope of eternal life.   **Titus 3:5-7**

And one thing more: Prepare a guest room for me, because I hope to be restored to you in answer to your prayers.   **Philemon 1:22**

But Christ is faithful as a son over God's house. And we are his house, if we hold on to our courage and the hope of which we boast.   **Hebrews 3:6**

We want each of you to show this same diligence to the very end, in order to make your hope sure.   **Hebrews 6:11**

God did this so that, by two unchangeable things in which it is impossible for God to lie, we who have fled to take hold of the hope offered to us may be greatly encouraged. We have this hope as an anchor for the soul, firm and secure.   **Hebrews 6:18-19**

The former regulation is set aside because it was weak and useless (for the law made nothing perfect), and a better hope is introduced, by which we draw near to God.   **Hebrews 7:18-19**

Let us hold unswervingly to the hope we profess, for he who promised us is faithful.   **Hebrews 10:23**

Now faith is being sure of what we hope for and certain of what we do not see.   **Hebrews 11:1**

Praise be to the God and Father of our Lord Jesus Christ! In his great mercy he has given us new birth into a living hope through the resurrection of Jesus Christ from the dead, and into an inheritance that can never perish, spoil or fade—kept in heaven for you, who through faith are shielded by God's power until the coming of the salvation that is ready to be revealed in the last time.   **1 Peter 1:3-5**

Therefore, prepare your minds for action; be self-controlled; set your hope fully on the grace to be given you when Jesus Christ is revealed.
                    1 Peter 1:13

Through him you believe in God, who raised him from the dead and glorified him, so that your faith and hope are in God.   **1 Peter 1:21**

For this is the way the holy women of the past who put their hope in God used to make themselves beautiful.   **1 Peter 3:5**

But in your hearts set apart Christ as Lord. Always be prepared to give an answer to everyone who asks you to give the reason for the hope that you have.   **1 Peter 3:15**

Everyone who has this hope in him purifies himself, just as he is pure.
1 John 3:3

I have much to write to you, but I do not want to use paper and ink. Instead, I hope to visit you and talk with you face to face, so that our joy may be complete.   **2 John 1:12**

I hope to see you soon, and we will talk face to face.   **3 John 1:14**

ONE
Hope Is Everywhere

1. John Peters and John Nichol, *Tornado Down* (London: Signet, 1993), 105-106.
2. Vaclav Havel, *Disturbing the Peace* (New York: Vintage, 1991), 181.
3. Havel, 181.
4. Martin E.P. Seligman, *Learned Optimism: How to Change Your Mind and Your Life* (New York: Pocket Books, 1990), 172.
5. Cited in Elizabeth Sherrill, *Prayer Calendar*, (February 1993), 38.
6. Michael F. Scheier and C.S. Carver, "Dispositional Optimism and Recovery from Coronary Bypass Surgery: The Beneficial Effects on Physical and Psychological Well-being," *Journal of Personality and Social Psychology*, 57 (1987): 1024-1040.
7. David G. Myers, *The Pursuit of Happiness: Who Is Happy—and Why* (New York: William Morrow & Company, 1992), 77.
8. Seligman, 76-79, 174-178.
9. Bruno Klopfer, "Psychological Variables in Human Cancer," *Journal of Projectional Techniques XII* (1957): 331-340.
10. C.R. Snyder, *The Psychology of Hope* (New York: The Free Press, 1994), 10.
11. Snyder, 26.
12. Snyder, 4.

TWO
The Revolution of Judaism

1. Denis Praeger, "Multi-culturalism and the War Against Western Values," lecture, October 7, 1991.
2. Leo Baech, "The Religion of the Hebrews," in Carl Clemen, General Editor, *Religions of the World: Their Nature and Their History* (Freeport, N.Y.: Books for Libraries Press, 1931), 22.
3. Baech, 23.
4. Baech, 17.
5. Baech, 18.
6. Milton Steinberg, *Basic Judaism* (New York: Harcourt, Brace & Company, 1965), 53.
7. Steinberg, 54.
8. Rabbi Chaim Asa, interview with Lela Gilbert, 1993.
9. Baech, 31.
10. Cited in Hans-Joachim Schoeps, "Judaism," *The Religions of Mankind* (New York: Doubleday, 1966), 211.
11. Rabbi Osrael Kelemer, Congregation Mogen David, West Los Angeles, interview with Lela Gilbert, 1993.
12. Kelemer.
13. Leo Baech, *The Essence of Judaism* (New York: Schocken, 1961), 15.
14. Kelemer interview.
15. Asa interview.
16. Kelemer interview.

204 Hope: The Heart's Great Quest

FOUR
Hope in Other Faiths

1. There is nevertheless a school of Japanese Buddhism, the Jodo School, founded in the twelfth century by the monk Honen, that developed such an extreme doctrine of faith as the sole basis of salvation that virtually no one who adopted it would be without some sort of theological hope. One of his disciples, Shinran, took this view to such an extreme that he came up with the formulation, "Even a good man will be received in Buddha's land, how much more a bad man." See Christmas Humphreys, *Buddhism* (Harmondsworth, England: Penguin, 1962), 177.
2. Geoffrey Parrinder, ed., *World Religions: From Ancient History to the Present* (New York: Hamlyn, 1971), 245.
3. "Hinduism" in *New Encyclopaedia Britannica,* 15th ed. Macropaedia, 30 vols. (Chicago: Helen Hemingway Benton, 1977), vol. 8, 889.
4. Juan Mascaro, trans., *The Upanishads* (Harmondsworth, England: Penguin, 1965), 13.
5. In the Introduction to Swami Prabhavanda and Christopher Isherwood, *The Song of God: Bhagavad-Gita* (New York: New American Library, 1954), 12.
6. *Bhagavad-Gita,* 51.
7. *The Upanishads,* 140.
8. *The Upanishads,* 140-141.
9. "Hinduism," *New Encyclopaedia Britannica,* 15th ed., vol. 8, 889.
10. *Bhagavad-Gita,* 133.
11. *Bhagavad-Gita,* 15-16. "Thou art that" is the translation of the Sanskrit *Tat tvam asi,* considered by many scholars of Hindus as the definitive answer to the question, "What is God?" This is the answer given by one of the sages in *The Upanishads.* See *The Upanishads,* 12.
12. *The Upanishads,* 24.
13. *Bhagavad-Gita,* 16.
14. *Bhagavad-Gita,* 16.
15. *The Upanishads,* 12.
16. *The Upanishads,* 90.
17. *The Upanishads,* 103.
18. *The Upanishads,* 103.
19. *The Upanishads,* 104.
20. John Ankerberg and John Weldon, *The Facts on Hinduism* (Eugene, Ore.: Harvest House, 1991), 29.
21. Ankerberg and Weldon, 20.
22. *Bhagavad-Gita,* 14.
23. *Bhagavad-Gita,* 32-33.
24. *Bhagavad-Gita,* 41.
25. Irwin Edman, (Introduction) *Marcus Aurelius and His Times* (Roslyn, N.Y.: Walter J. Black Inc., 1945), 61.
26. *Bhagavad-Gita,* 46-47.
27. *Bhagavad-Gita,* 48.
28. Christmas Humphreys, *Buddhism* (Harmondsworth, England: Penguin, 1962), 25.
29. Humphreys, 11.

30. Cited in Humphreys, 17.
31. Humphreys, 79.
32. Edward Conze, *Buddhism: Its Essence and Development* (New York: Harper and Row, 1959), 53.
33. Humphreys, 248. The Eightfold Path consists of right motive, right speech, right acts, right livelihood, right effort, right concentration, and *samadhi* (Sanskrit for "transic concentration").
34. Humphreys, 123.
35. Conze, 18.
36. Humphreys, 19.
37. Humphreys, 74.
38. Conze, 40.
39. Conze, 53-54.
40. Conze, 53.
41. Conze, 17.
42. Cited in Humphreys, 123-124.
43. Conze, 21.
44. Humphreys, 76.
45. Conze, 22.
46. Humphreys, 76.
47. Humphreys, 53, and Conze, 117.
48. Conze, 189.
49. Edward Conze, trans., *Buddhist Scriptures* (Harmondsworth, England: Penguin, 1959), 89.
50. Hans-Joachim Schoeps, *The Religions of Mankind, Their Origin and Development* (Garden City, NY: Doubleday, 1961), 170-171.
51. Alfred Guillame, *Islam* (Harmondsworth, England: Penguin, 1956), 194.
52. Thomas W. Lippman, *Understanding Islam* (New York: New American Library, 1982), 11.
53. N.J. Dawood, trans., *The Koran* (Harmondsworth, England: Penguin, 1956), 140.
54. *The Koran,* 18.
55. *The Koran,* 29.
56. *The Koran,* 374.
57. *The Koran,* 18, and passim.
58. *The Koran,* 211.
59. *The Koran,* 36.
60. *The Koran,* 17.
61. *The Koran,* 106-107.
62. *The Koran,* 112.
63. Schoeps, 235-237.
64. William M. Miller, *A Christian's Response to Islam* (Wheaton, Ill.: Tyndale, 1976), 83-84.
65. Guillaume, 120.
66. Guillaume, 120-121.
67. Ibn Khaldun, *An Introduction to History: The Muqaddimah* (London: Routledge and Kegan Paul, 1978), 257-258.
68. Parrinder, 495.
69. Guillaume, 149-150.

70. John Williams, *Islam* (New York: Washington Square Press, 1963), 139.
71. Guillaume, 150.

FIVE
The Enlightenment and the Seeds of False Hope

1. A point made in Walter Martin, *The New Age Cult* (Minneapolis: Bethany House, 1989), 13.
2. George Carey, *I Believe in Man* (London: Hodder and Stoughton, 1977), 174-175.
3. Albert Schweitzer, *The Quest for the Historical Jesus* (London: Adam and Charles Black, 1954), 40.
4. In a striking parallel, Chinese pro-democracy activist students in Beijing brought a statue of the "Goddess of Democracy" into Tiananmen Square just days before the brutal crackdown on demonstrations by the Chinese army on June 4, 1989. Because the "goddess" many of the students had idolized failed to hold back the tanks of repression, Chinese university students in significant numbers began to take an interest in the Christian faith in the weeks and months after the massacre.
5. Cited in Walter Kauffmann, *Hegel: A Reinterpretation* (Notre Dame, Ind.: University of Notre Dame Press, 1978), 13-14.
6. Cited in Vincent P. Miceli, *The Gods of Atheism* (New Rochelle, N.Y.: Arlington House, 1971), i.
7. A. Robert Caponigri, *Philosophy from the Romantic Age to the Age of Positivism* (Notre Dame: University of Notre Dame Press, 1971), 4.
8. Georg W.F. Hegel, *Early Theological Writings* (Chicago, Ill.: University of Chicago Press, 1948), 170.
9. Hegel, 276
10. Kauffmann, 32-33.
11. Kauffmann, 34.
12. Kauffmann, 35.
13. A major intellectual debate broke out in 1989 after the lead article in the respected and influential Washington-based international affairs quarterly *The National Interest* published an article by scholar and former State Department official, Francis Fukuyama, entitled "The End of History." The article argued that, with the collapse of Communism in Eastern Europe, the Hegelian dialectic had now run its course: Democracy was the final historical form of politics and had essentially triumphed globally. The fierce barrage of objections to this position demonstrated how powerfully the entire Hegelian idea of the dialectic has captured the imagination, if not the intellects, of Western intellectuals.
14. Cited in Robert Tucker, *Philosophy and Myth in Karl Marx* (Cambridge: Cambridge University Press, 1972), 64.
15. Hegel, *Encyclopedia*, as quoted in Kaufmann, *Hegel: A Re-interpretation*, 272-273.
16. Henrich Leo, *Die Hegelingen* (Halle, Germany: 1838), as quoted in Karl Marx and Frederick Engels, *Collected Works* (London: Lawrence & Wishart, 1975), vol. 2, 600, footnote 49.
17. Marx and Engels, vol. 2, 321.
18. Marx and Engels, vol. 3, 464.
19. As quoted in Miceli, 33.

20. Miceli, 33.
21. Heinrich Heine, *Geschichte der Religion und Philosophie in Deutschland* (Berlin: 1834, 28), as quoted in Karl Lowith, *From Hegel to Nietzsche: The Revolution in Nineteenth Century Thought* (New York: Holt, Rinehart and Winston, 1964), 44.
22. As quoted in Henri de Lubac, *The Drama of Atheist Humanism* (New York: New American Library, 1963), 22.

SIX
Hegel, Marx, Humanism, and Freud

1. Marx and Engels, vol. 5, 8.
2. Marx makes this argument forcefully and at great length in his *Notebooks on Epicurean Philosophy*, written in preparation for his doctoral dissertation but not published during his lifetime. See *Collected Works*, vol. 1, 405, 514.
3. David McLellan, *Karl Marx: Early Texts* (Oxford: Basil Blackwell, 1972), 19-20.
4. Karl Marx and Friedrich Engels, *The Communist Manifesto* (New York: International Publishers, 1948), 44.
5. Richard Crossman, ed., *The God That Failed* (New York: Bantam, 1965), 66.
6. Paul Hollander, *Political Pilgrims* (New York: Oxford University Press, 1981).
7. Sidney Rittenberg and Amanda Bennett, *The Man Who Stayed Behind* (New York: Simon and Schuster, 1993), 73.
8. As quoted in R.N. Carew Hunt, *The Theory and Practice of Communism* (Harmondsworth, England: Penguin, 1963), 106.
9. *Quotations from Chairman Mao Tse-Tung* (Peking [Beijing]: Foreign Languages Press, 1966).
10. George Urban, ed., *The Miracles of Chairman Mao* (London: Tom Stacey, 1971), 9.
11. Urban, xiv.
12. Nien Cheng, *Life and Death in Shanghai* (New York: Penguin, 1988), 249.
13. *New Programme and New Constitution of the Revolutionary Communist Party, USA* (Chicago: RCP, 1981), 6.
14. Charles Darwin, *The Descent of Man and Selection in Relation to Sex* (Chicago: 1990), *Great Books of the Western World*, vol. 43, 597.
15. Jacob Bronowsky, *The Ascent of Man* (1973), as quoted in Francis Schaeffer, *How Should We Then Live?* (Old Tappan, N.J.: Revell, 1976), 150.
16. Paul Kurtz, *In Defense of Secular Humanism* (Buffalo, N.Y.: Prometheus Books, 1983), 8.
17. Kurtz, 41. The signatories included such outstanding international intellectuals as Russian nuclear scientist and dissident Andrei Sakharov, American science fiction author Isaac Asimov, and British biologist Sir Julian Huxley.
18. Kurtz, 40.
19. Kurtz, 42.
20. Kurtz, 5.
21. Friedrich Nietzsche, *Beyond Good and Evil: Prelude to a Philosophy of the Future* (Chicago: 1990) *Great Books of the Western World*, vol. 43, 483.
22. Nietzsche, 485.
23. Kurtz, 40.

24. Kurtz, 41.
25. H.G. Wells, *The Mind at the End of its Tether* as quoted in Herbert Schlossberg, *Idols for Destruction: Christian Faith and Its Confrontation with American Society* (Nashville, Tenn.: Nelson, 1983), 2.
26. Bertrand Russell, *Why I Am Not a Christian* (New York: Simon and Schuster, 1957), 107.
27. Paul C. Vitz, *Psychology as Religion: The Cult of Self-Worship* (Grand Rapids, Mich.: William B. Eerdmans, 1994), xii.
28. Sigmund Freud, *Beyond the Pleasure Principle* (Chicago, 1990), *Great Books of the Western World*, vol. 54, 654.
29. Freud, 787.
30. Freud, 802.

SEVEN
Gnosticism, Self-Worship, and the New Age

1. Elaine Pagels, *The Gnostic Gospels* (New York: Random , 1979), xx-xxi.
2. Pagels, xxxv.
3. Richard Noll, "The Rose, the Cross and the Analyst" in *The New York Times,* 15 October 1994, A26.
4. As quoted in Vitz, *Psychology as Religion*, 6.
5. Vitz, 45.
6. As quoted by James Hitchcock in *What Is Secular Humanism?* (Ann Arbor, Mich.: Servant, 1982), 128.
7. Vitz, 52.
8. Cited in Vitz, 100.
9. Harry Emerson Fosdick, *On Being a Real Person*, as quoted in Vitz, 100.
10. John Ankerberg and John Weldon, *The New Age Movement* (Eugene, Ore.: Harvest House, 1988), 25.
11. Napoleon Hill, *Think and Grow Rich* (Ballantine, 1983), 50, 168.
12. Vitz, 102.
13. Norman Vincent Peale, *The Power of Positive Thinking* (London: William Heinemann Limited, 1952), 1.
14. See especially Norman Vincent Peale, *The Tough-Minded Optimist* (Englewood Cliffs, N.J.: Prentice-Hall, 1961), passim.
15. Ankerberg and Weldon, 25.
16. Robert H. Schuller, *Success Is Never Ending, Failure Is Never Final* (New York: Bantam, 1990), n.p.
17. Vitz, 96-97.
18. Gloria Steinem, *Revolution from Within: A Book of Self-Esteem* (Boston: Little, Brown and Company, 1992), 30-31.
19. Steinem, 32.
20. Steinem, 153.
21. Steinem, 310.
22. Steinem, 325.
23. Vitz, 27.

24. See especially Douglas R. Groothuis, *Unmasking the New Age* (Downers Grove, Ill.: InterVarsity Press, 1986); Walter Martin, *The New Age Cult* (Minneapolis: Bethany House, 1989); Russell Chandler, *Understanding the New Age* (Dallas: Word Publishing, 1988); John Ankerberg and John Weldon, *The New Age Movement* (Eugene, Ore.: Harvest House, 1988).
25. Margot Adler, *Drawing Down the Moon: Witches, Druids, Goddess-Worshipers and Other Pagans in America Today* (Boston: Beacon, 1979), cited in Groothuis, *Unmasking the New Age*, 138.
26. Shirley MacLaine, *Dancing in the Light* (New York: Bantam, 1983), 183, as quoted in Vitz, 125.
27. See especially Chapter 14 of the recent work by Joscelyn Godwin, *The Theosophical Enlightenment* (Albany, N.Y.: State University of New York Press, 1994).
28. As quoted in Peter Jones, *The Gnostic Empire Strikes Back* (Phillipsburg, N.J.: P&R, 1992), 50.
29. Godwin, *The Theosophical Enlightenment*, 379.
30. Shirley MacLaine, *Going Within: A Guide for Inner Transformation* (New York: Bantam, 1988), 189, as quoted in Jones, 14.
31. As quoted in Martin, 26.
32. When the author was reporting on a story in the Philippines for *Time* in 1975 on faith healing (in this case, healing through spiritist occult powers), he encountered a Filipino family involved in spiritism upon whose youngest child a medium put a curse when the father refused to permit the teaching of reincarnation during a channeling session. The child, about four years old at the time, died of an undiagnosable fever. The family subsequently became Christian and immediately grasped the difference between occult and Holy Spirit-endowed supernatural powers.
33. Cited in Ankerberg and Weldon, 12.
34. As quoted in Groothuis, 144.
35. Groothuis, 153.
36. Helen Schucman, *A Course in Miracles* (Glen Ellen, Calif.: Foundations for Inner Peace, 1992).

EIGHT
True Hope and the Messiah

1. *Interpreter's Dictionary of the Bible* (New York: Abingdon, 1962), 640.
2. Edward W. Goodrick and John R. Kohlenberger III, eds., *The NIV Exhaustive Concordance* (Grand Rapids, Mich.: Zondervan, 1990).
3. *Interpreter's Dictionary of the Bible*, 643.
4. Great benefit and understanding of the way faith-filled praise can actually alter adverse circumstances themselves can be derived from the inspiring books by former U.S. military chaplain Merlin Carothers on the subject of praise. His *Prison to Praise* (Escondido, Calif.: Merlin R. Carothers, 1970) is one of the classics of understanding the relationship of faith and praise to adversity and suffering.
5. *Sacramentum Mundi: Encyclopedia of Theology* (New York: Herder and Herder, 1969), vol. 3, 532.

6. Gerhard Kittel, ed., *Theological Dictionary of the New Testament* (Grand Rapids, Mich.: Eerdmans, 1967), 532.
7. *Interpreter's Dictionary of the Bible*, 643.

NINE
Hope and the Christian Mystery

1. Cyril R. Richardson, ed., *Early Christian Fathers* (New York: Macmillan, 1970), 56.
2. Richardson, 67.
3. Richardson, 337.
4. "Hope" in *The New Catholic Encyclopedia* (New York: McGraw-Hill, 1967), vol. 7, 779.
5. "Hope" in *The New Catholic Encyclopedia*, 779.
6. Joseph Pieper, *On Hope* (San Francisco: Ignatius, 1986), 69-70.
7. Thomas Aquinas, *Summa Theologica* (Chicago, 1990), *Great Books of the Western World*, vol. 18, 85.
8. Thomas Aquinas, vol. 18, 70.
9. As quoted in Pieper, 35.
10. Pieper, 137.
11. Pieper, 137.
12. *Great Books of the Western World*, vol. 19, 122.
13. "Hope" in *The New Catholic Encyclopedia*, vol. 1, 138.
14. Pieper, 72.
15. Pieper, 87.
16. Pieper, 88.
17. Pieper, 47.
18. Pieper, 48.
19. Pieper, 57, 60.
20. Pieper, 60.
21. Pieper, 71.
22. Robert Royal, "The Literary Value of Hope: Péguy's Porche du mystère de la deuxième vertu," in manuscript galleys of article made available to author, 180.
23. Royal, 181.
24. Royal, 160.
25. Royal, 161.
26. Royal, 178-179.
27. Royal, 165.
28. Royal, 173.
29. Royal, 162.
30. John Paul II, *Crossing the Threshold of Hope* (New York: Afred A. Knopf, 1994).
31. John Paul II, viii.
32. John Paul II, 20.
33. John Paul II, 22.
34. John Paul II, 125.
35. As quoted in Jurgen Moltmann, *Theology of Hope: On the Ground and Implications of a Christian Eschatology* (New York: Harper and Row, 1965), 19.
36. Moltmann, 20.

37. *The Book of Common Prayer* (New York: The Church Hymnal Corporation, 1979), 223.
38. *The Book of Common Prayer*, 236.
39. *The Book of Common Prayer*, 246-247.
40. *The Book of Common Prayer*, 501.
41. *The Book of Common Prayer*, 861-862.
42. Moltmann, 20.
43. Moltmann, 32.
44. Moltmann, 34-35.
45. Emil Brunner, *Faith, Hope and Love* (Philadelphia: Westminster, 1956), 43.
46. Brunner, 50.
47. Dietrich and Alice Von Hildebrand, *The Art of Living* (Manchester, N.H.: Sophia Institute Press, 1994), 91.
48. Von Hildebrand, 79-80.
49. Von Hildebrand, 6.
50. Von Hildebrand, 43.
51. Von Hildebrand, 40-51, passim.
52. Carl F. Henry, *The Twilight of a Great Civilization: The Drift Towards Neo-Paganism* (Westchester, Ill.: Crossway, 1988), 35-36.
53. Billy Graham, *Decision Magazine*, September 1993, 3.
54. Brunner, 57.
55. Von Hildebrand, 81.
56. Von Hildebrand, 85.
57. Leanne Payne, "Pastoral Care Ministries," Summer 1993, 2-3.
58. Eugene Petersen, *The Message* (Colorado Springs, Colo.: NavPress, 1993).
59. Eugene Peterson, *A Long Obedience in the Same Direction* (Downer's Grove, Ill.: InterVarsity Press, 1980).
60. David B. Barrett, ed., *World Christian Encyclopedia* (Nairobi: Oxford University Press, 1982), 370.

TEN

The Puritans: Hope and History

1. J.I. Packer, *A Quest for Godliness: The Puritan Vision of the Christian Life* (Wheaton, Ill.: Crossway, 1990), 11.
2. Richard Hofstadter, *Anti-Intellectualism in American Life* (New York: Vintage, 1963), 59-60.
3. Roger Sharrock, in Introduction to a paperback edition of John Bunyan, *Pilgrim's Progress* (Harmondsworth, England: Penguin, 1965), 13.
4. Packer, 22.
5. Iain H. Murray, *The Puritan Hope: A Study in Revival and the Interpretation of Prophecy* (Edinburgh: Banner of Truth, 1971), xxi-xxii.
6. Packer, 233.
7. Bunyan, 156.
8. William Gurnall, *The Christian in Complete Armour* (Lindale, Tex.: World Challenge, 1983), vol. 3, 172, 174.
9. As quoted in Murray, 91.

10. Murray, 94-95.
11. Murray, 92.
12. Murray, 92.
13. Murray, 102.
14. As quoted in J.H. Merle D'Aubigne, *The Protector* (Harrisonburg, Va.: Sprinkle, 1983), 197.
15. D'Aubigne, 268-269.
16. As quoted in D'Aubigne, 273.
17. As quoted in Murray, 253-254.
18. John Preston, *The Breast-Plate of Faith and Love* (London: Nicholas Bourne, 1634, and Carlisle, Penn.: Banner of Truth, 1979), 229.
19. Preston, 231.
20. As quoted in Packer, 181.
21. Gurnall, vol. 3, 175.
22. Packer, 323.
23. Packer, 326.
24. Murray, 97.
25. President Clinton's State of the Union address, January 24, 1995, drew special attention to two African-American clergy, John and Diana Cherry of the AME Zion Church in Temple Hills, Maryland. President Clinton praised the Revs. Cherry for focusing much of their pastoral work on keeping families together.
26. In 1949, when China's population was about 559 million, China's Protestant and Roman Catholic Christian population was estimated at around four million. In 1992, an unofficial figure leaked from Chinese statistical sources in Beijing estimated the total number of Protestant and Roman Catholic Christians at around 75 million. Other estimates have ranged from 20 million to 60 million. Even if the lowest possible figure of 20 million is selected, that is a fivefold increase in Christians while the natural population increase has been twofold. China's population in 1995 is estimated at 1.2 billion.
27. Murray, 258.
28. As quoted in Murray, 200.
29. As quoted in Murray, 186.
30. Gurnall, vol. 3, 175.
31. Gurnall, vol. 3, 183.
32. Gurnall, vol. 3, 177.
33. Gurnall, vol. 3, 196.

ELEVEN
The Fruits of Hope

1. Bill Beutel, "At That Very Moment," *Guideposts,* January 1993, 3.
2. Beutel, 6.
3. Dorothy Dudley Muth, "My Rainbow Covenant," *Guideposts,* August 1993, 37.
4. Conversation with the author, April 1993.
5. Viktor Frankl, *Man's Search for Meaning* (New York: Pocket Books, 1984), 95.
6. Frankl, 97.
7. Frankl, 102-104 passim.

8. Irina Ratushinksaya, *Grey Is the Color of Hope* (New York: Alfred A. Knopf, 1989), 356.
9. Armando Vallodares, *Against All Hope: The Prison Memoirs of Armando Vallodares* (New York: Knopf, 1986).
10. Jurgen Moltmann, *The Experiment Hope* (Philadelphia: Fortress, 1975), 85.
11. East Gates Ministries International, *Seeing Beyond the Impossible,* report entitled "God Put Me in School," 1993.
12. *The New York Times,* November 28, 1993, 1.
13. Doug Warner in conversation with the author, Virginia Beach, October 27, 1993.
14. Moltmann, 32-35 passim.
15. "Hope" in the *New Catholic Encyclopedia,* vol. 1, 138.
16. Robert F. Kennedy, speech at Capetown University, June 6, 1966.
17. Michele Clark, in conversation with the author, October 1993.
18. Norman Vincent Peale, "How to Get Hope," *Guideposts,* January 1987, 6.
19. Peale, 6-8.
20. Gurnall, 205.
21. R.P. Hromas, *Passport to the Bible* (Wheaton, Ill.: Tyndale, 1983), 11, and in conversation with the author.
22. Gurnall, 211.
23. Gurnall, 214-217, passim.
24. Gurnall, 208-209.
25. Gurnall, 210.
26. Pieper, 71.
27. Henri J.M. Nouwen, *With Open Hands* (Notre Dame, Ind.: Ave Maria, 1972), 76.
28. Nouwen, 78.
29. Nouwen, 76.
30. Nouwen, 82.
31. Catherine Marshall, *Guideposts,* March 1993, 14 (originally appeared in October, 1960).
32. Eugene Petersen, *A Long Obedience in the Same Direction,* 133.
33. Petersen, 138-139, passim.
34. Petersen, 140.
35. Nouwen, 85.